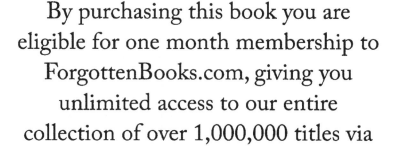

ISBN 978-0-656-82830-2
PIBN 10493014

THE

Presbytery of Washington City

AND

THE CHURCHES UNDER ITS CARE.

Prepared for the Centennial of the General Assembly,
May 17, 1888, by order of the Presbytery, in
response to the Resolution of
the Assembly.

J. E. NOURSE,
B. F. BITTINGER, D. D., } Committee.
JOHN CHESTER, D. D.,

WASHINGTON:
Gibson Bros., Printers and Bookbinders.
1888.

The Churches.

Suburban Churches.

Frontispiece.

BRIDGE STREET CHURCH.   ERECTED 1782; REBUILT 1821; TAKEN DOWN 1872.

The Centennial of the Assembly.

The 100th meeting of the General Assembly of the Presbyterian Church in the United States, to be held in Philadelphia in May, 1888, is looked for with much interest. It will be a grateful remembrance of its organization, and of a century of God's favor to the churches under its care. In accordance with the unvaried custom of the Church, the Assembly of the Church North will meet on the third Thursday of May, this year the 17th; on the 24th, the Assembly of the Church South will unite with it in celebrating the organization of the First Assembly in 1789.

The memorials of these meetings will record themselves in the enlarged and consecrated contributions of the year for the promotion of the Redeemer's kingdom.

Within the arrangements for this observance, adopted by the Assembly of the Church North, is the presentation by each Synod, Presbytery, and Church, of a history of its founding and growth.

The Presbytery of Washington City cordially responds to the call of the Assembly. It recognizes the founding of Presbyterianism in this District, and its vicinity, as effected more than a quarter of a century before its occupancy for the seat of the Government, and the growth of our Churches as emphasized by their influence on the many leading minds gathered from time to time in council at the National Capital. A number of our Presidents, members of their Cabinets, very many Senators and Repsentatives, members of the Supreme Judiciary, and Officers of the Army and Navy have been and are attendants or members of our Churches, and several of our pastors have been Chaplains to the Congresses. The influence, thus hopefully exerted on minds which guide the nation, is beyond our estimate.

The Records of the large extension * of the whole Church, and

---

* "At the first meeting of the General Assembly, held May 21, 1789, the Church consisted of but 177 Ministers, 431 Churches, and about 18,000 Communicants. It contributed to the cause of Missions, $852.00. The rolls reported to the Assembly of the Church North in 1887 give the number of Ministers, 5,654; of Churches, 6,436; of Communicants, 696,767. The benevolent contributions of the year had been about $3,198,458. From 1789 to 1887 the aggregate of contributions of the whole Church North and South had been about $67,000,000, of which $48,704,209 have been given since 1870. The total of additions to membership by confession of faith since 1789 have been about

those of its lower courts and Churches are made to the praise only of the grace of God, the Giver; and while we may not glorify the men who under Him have planted and sustained the Churches, we rightfully commemorate their memories by the record of the work given into their hands.

The calls of the Assembly and the Presbytery may be met by presenting in brief a Record—

I. Of the connection of the Churches first planted here with the earliest organization covering this section of the country.

II. Of the organization and work of each of the two Presbyteries now consolidated, the District of Columbia and the Potomac.

III. Of the work of the existing Presbytery; and

IV. Of the founding and growth of each of its Churches.

The Churches now under the care of the Presbytery, named in the order of their respective organizations, are:

The BLADENSBURG, now HYATTSVILLE, Maryland, organized in 1718; FIRST ALEXANDRIA, 1772; BRIDGE STREET, now WEST STREET, 1780; FIRST PRESBYTERIAN, Washington, 1795; F. STREET, 1803, united with the SECOND PRESBYTERIAN of 1820, in the NEW YORK AVE. (1859); FOURTH CHURCH, 1828; FIFTEENTH ST., 1841; NEELSVILLE, Maryland, 1845; LEWINSVILLE, Virginia, 1846; FIRST PRINCE WILLIAM, Virginia, 1850; ASSEMBLY's, Washington, March 9, 1853; SIXTH, March 30, 1853; SEVENTH CHURCH, now WESTMINSTER, June, 1853; WESTERN, 1855; DARNESTOWN, Maryland, 1857; Church on Capitol Hill, now METROPOLITAN, 1864; NORTH CHURCH, 1865; MANASSAS, Virginia, 1867; CLIFTON, 1870; FALLS CHURCH, February, 1873; VIENNA, November, 1873; HERMON, Maryland, 1874; EASTERN, Washington, 1875; BOYD STATION, Maryland, 1877; UNITY, Washington, 1882; CHURCH OF THE COVENANT, 1885.

1,500,000 " (Epitome of the History of the Church by Stated Clerk, W. H. Roberts).

At the organization of the Church South it had 10 Synods, 47 Presbyteries, 1,000 Churches, and 75,000 Communicants. To these were added in 1863 the "United Synod of the South" bringing 12,000 Communicants; in 1867, the Presbytery of Patapsco with 575, and in 1867, part of the Synod of Kentucky with 13,540; a total of 110,115 Communicants. The rolls reported to the Assembly South in 1887 numbered 13 Synods, 69 Presbyteries, 2,236 Churches, and 150,398 members. The total membership of the Presbyterian Church in the United States is, therefore, a little more than 846,000. For which to God be all the glory.

To which list are to be added those of the Churches among the Freedmen, in Amelia County, Virginia: BIG OAK and MOUNT ZION, in 1866; RUSSELL GROVE, 1868; ALBRIGHT, 1871; OAK GROVE, 1881; MOUNT HERMON, 1882. Of none of these have definite accounts been found available for record beyond these dates.

Of the roll first given separate sketches are offered, those in the same field being taken together, as associate Churches.

For the basis of the papers, acknowledgments are due to Rev. Drs. SUNDERLAND, BITTINGER and CHESTER, for the histories read by them at the Centennial of Baltimore Presbytery, 1886; to Dr. SUNDERLAND, for the loan of the valued, though unfinished, manuscript history, written by the late Rev. Mr. McFALLS; to Dr. BITTINGER, for his Journal of the Churches, to the year 1879; and to the officers of the Sessions, who have revised the sketches presented.

The hope is entertained that these memorials of God's goodly favor to His people may, in the hands of church officers and private members, further promote Christian activity and fellowship.

J. E. N.

1. The Churches First Planted in this Region under the Earliest Organization Covering It.

From Dr. Hodge's "Constitutional History" it will be learned that the three Presbyterian Ministers, Rev. Isaac Keith, S. B. Balch, and James Hunt, who first labored in this section of the country, were members first of the old Presbytery of Donegal, Pennsylvania, which covered a widely extended territory. The earliest of our organizations in this region were under its authority. In 1786 these, with Dr. Patrick Alison, Revs. John Slemons and George Luckey; Elders Captain Joshua Beall, of Bladensburg; Dr. William Lyon, of Baltimore, and the vacant Churches of the territory, were set off by the Synod of New York and Philadelphia to form the Presbytery of Baltimore. Until the year 1823 the Churches of First Alexandria, Bridge Street, First and Second Presbyterian, Washington; Bladensburg, Cabin John and Bethesda, in Maryland, were under the care of that Presbytery.

Even a passing review of this period of 37 years would exhibit some impressive facts. The men who founded the earliest of our organizations were called to a full missionary work. This region was, in their day, as purely missionary ground as now is any in the far West—their s, the labor of the pioneer. Balch, journeying from his Church in Georgetown to found that of Frederick and others, and Brackenridge, crossing from Cabin John to Bladensburg, and the devout Elders who collected funds for the erection of the First Presbyterian of 1795, must have known something of frontier travel. They were men of strong convictions of duty to both church and state, sharing the principles of our Witherspoon, and receiving the scantiest ministerial support.

The evidences of the manifestation of that characteristic of our Church—a liberal feeling towards all other evangelical denominations—are as clear. Dr. Hodge's history records this in full as shown to our kindred Churches in the mother country. A like manifestation towards the Congregational Church in the United States brought about the "Plan of Union" of 1801. In 1824 it brought the F Street Church from the Associate Reformed Body into the District of Columbia Presbytery.

II. The Presbytery of the District of Columbia.—1823-1870.

At its session of October, 1823, the Synod of Philadelphia created the new Presbytery of the District of Columbia, on the petition of the Baltimore Presbytery for a division—a request arising out of a courteous deference to the wishes, but also to the growing needs, of the Churches of the District. The population of the national capital had steadily increased, the country had become settled from the disquietude of the two wars through which the Churches with it had passed, and the pastoral ministrations of the city had been those of increasing promise. In Georgetown, Dr. BALCH was gaining on the hearts of the people; in Washington, Drs. POST and BAKER were receiving many accessions to their Churches as the fruits of pulpit ministration and frequent pastoral visitations, together with the time-honored custom, then, by necessity, happily in use, of prayer meetings held in the homes of the congregations. It will be noticed that, in the new organization, a missionary spirit remembered the wants of the surrounding country districts.

The Synod's order was that the Presbytery should consist of the following Ministers and Churches, to be set off from the Presbytery of Baltimore, viz:

Rev. STEPHEN B. BALCH, Pastor of the BRIDGE-STREET CHURCH, Georgetown; Rev. REUBEN POST, of the FIRST CHURCH, Washington; Rev. JOHN BRECKENRIDGE, stated supply of the BLADENSBURG CHURCH; Rev. ELIAS HARRISON, Pastor of the FIRST CHURCH, Alexandria; Rev. DANIEL BAKER, of the SECOND CHURCH, Washington; Rev. JOHN MINES, Pastor of CABIN JOHN and BETHESDA, Maryland; Rev. JOHN N. CAMPBELL, assistant of Dr. BALCH; and Rev. WILLIAM MAFFIT, Principal of a school in Fairfax county, Virginia. Three licentiates, Messrs. A. BELT, R. R. GURLEY, and S. TUSTIN, were placed under the care of the Presbytery.

At the first meeting of the new body held in Alexandria, May 11, 1824, the Ministers, except Messrs. MINES and MAFFIT, were present, with Ruling Elders, J. S. NEVIUS, DANIEL RICKETTS, JAMES MOORE, and JAMES S. HANDY. Rev. J. BRECKENRIDGE was elected Moderator. The membership of the Churches represented numbered 277.

In the first year of its organization the F STREET CHURCH of

Washington was received from the Second (Associate) Presbytery of Philadelphia, and the SECOND CHURCH of Alexandria from the Presbytery of Winchester; in 1829, the FOURTH CHURCH, Washington, then organized. Within the fourteen years following the formation of the Presbytery, were enrolled as members, Rev. Dr. JAMES LAURIE and Revs. WELLS ANDREWS, I. L. SKINNER, W. C. WALTON, J. N. DANFORTH, J. C. SMITH, MASON NOBLE, E. C. HUTCHINSON, Dr. W. HILL, and P. H. FOWLER. Nine Licentiates were under its care, the three already named, and Messrs. JOSHUA MOORE, EDWARD D. SMITH, ELIPHALET N. BOSWORTH, JAMES J. GRAEE, FLAVEL S. MINES, and WILLIAM McLAIN; of whom seven, and JAMES NOURSE, a graduate of Princeton Seminary, were ordained.

Six pastoral relations were constituted: For the SECOND ALEXANDRIA, two successively; for the SECOND CHURCH, Washington, one; for the FOURTH CHURCH, two; and for the FIRST CHURCH, one. Seven pastoral relations were dissolved. Ten ministers were dismissed to other bodies.

During the period named, the Presbytery went steadily forward in its appointed work, a number of conversions being reported from its Churches as the fruits of precious seasons of refreshing influence from on High. In the general spirit of activity in the Church at large—in the work of Missions, the Bible, Tract, and Temperance causes—it took commendable share; sound doctrinal preaching, catechetical instruction in the family and the Sabbath-Schools, and earnest pastoral work being largely owned by the Head of the Church. In its first Narrative, prepared for the General Assembly of 1824, the Presbytery stated with thankfulness the organization of a weekly prayer meeting held from Church to Church, conducted by the ministers in turn and that of two Sabbath-School Unions, one in Georgetown and one in Alexandria.

The General Assembly of 1836 transferred the Presbytery from the Synod of Philadelphia to that of Virginia. The membership of the Churches in that year was 1259. Two ministers had died, Rev. Professor MAFFIT in 1828 and Rev. Dr. BALCH in 1833.

The fuller work of the body was now, however, to be, at least partially, interrupted by the well known separation of the Church at large into the Old and the New School Assemblies; here into *the two Presbyteries—the Potomac and the District.*

For some years before the division of 1837–'38 just named, the views of many of the leading men in the whole Church had been steadily diverging on the chief points of doctrine and church polity which characterize Presbyterianism. Special objections were being more and more frequently and urgently raised, also against the further continuance of the old " Plan of Union of 1801 " with the Congregational Association of Connecticut, under which it was now claimed evils of magnitude in both doctrine and polity were steadily increasing to the injury of the Church at large.

Strong Synods, especially in Ohio and New York, had grown up under this plan by which the ministers of either body could serve in Churches of the other, the Churches being represented in Presbytery by either Elders or Committee men, as the case might be ; such representatives of the Presbyteries from Congregational Associations having seats in the General Assembly. When, in the logic of events, the " Old School " and the " New " extended themselves throughout the whole Church, the Presbytery of the District was found to embrace its share, though it was but a minority of the body. In 1839, therefore, when a vote was taken on receiving a Mandate from the Synod of Virginia requiring adherence to the acts of the Assembly of 1837–'38, which excinded several of the Northern Synods from the Church, the Presbytery divided, Messrs. LAURIE, HARRISON, BOSWORTH, and BRECKENRIDGE representing their Churches, and Rev. I. L. SKINNER and Rev. J. MCVEAN (without pastoral charges) withdrew from the body, declining its further jurisdiction.

The District Presbytery dropped these names from the rolls, but the General Assembly (O. S.) recognized them as the true body, of that name, which they retained until merged in 1841 in the Presbytery of Baltimore. In 1858 they were set off from that Presbytery to form the new one of the Presbytery of Potomac.

For nearly forty years, therefore, the anomalous condition of the churches here, so long previously united, was that of being from 1839 to 1841, some under one and some under the other of two bodies, each claiming the same old name—designated further as O. S. or N. S.—thence from 1841 to 1858, of some being under the Baltimore Presbytery O. S.; others under the District N. S.; and thence to the reunion of the whole church in 1870, of some being under the Presbytery of Potomac O. S., the majority under that of the District N. S.

From the date of the separation, the spirit of aggression and rivalry between these two bodies became apparent, especially, however, in a zeal for planting churches and establishing missionary posts. Continuing the history of the Presbytery of the District, it is found that in common with other churches at and near the seat of Government it passed through times of great excitements both in church and state.

The Mexican war, the discovery of gold, followed by the expansion of our territory, and with it the agitation of the slavery question—all exerted a powerful influence, felt more sensibly by the churches on the border line and at the centre of the nation than in other sections. During the long period of the years 1838 to the beginning of the war in 1861, despite these and other adverse circumstances, the Presbytery still put forth its vigorous efforts in church extension, and the number of its membership was largely increased.

The chief characteristics of these years were this marked activity in church extension, supported by earnest and sound pulpit and pastoral ministrations; the isolation of the body from ecclesiastical oversight from 1857 to 1862; its depression during the war; and its strong loyalty to the Union throughout that trying time.

The spirit of church extension was intensified by the meeting of the General Assembly N. S., in 1852, in Washington, when a new impulse in that direction was received from that body.

Isolation from Synodical oversight was effected as the result of the growing excitement on the slavery question. The Commissioners to the General Assembly meeting at Cleveland, in 1857, on the propositions being there made touching this subject, being under no instructions from their Presbytery, thought best to withdraw, and issued an appeal to the ministers to call a Convention looking towards a new organization. This resulted in the formation of the " Knoxville Synod." This action, sustained by the Synod of Virginia, and involving the separation of the District Presbytery from the Northern Church, was, however, " calmly and conscientiously " opposed by the pastors here, no representation from the Presbytery again appearing in the Synod. No church extension was possible during the war.

Between 1838 and 1857, eighteen ministers were received, viz: J. G. HAMNER, J. KNOX, W. T. SPROLE, H. H. MORGAN, T. L. HAMNER, S. MERRILL, E. BALLENTYNE, J. R. ECKARD, S. WASHBURNE, W. T. EVA, M. NOBLE, M. JEWELL, B. SUNDERLAND, A. D. HOLLISTER, E. J. NEWLIN, J. S. BARTLETT, H. DUNNING, W. T. CATTO. Twenty-three ministers were installed: J. C. SMITH, T. L. HAMNER, G. J. WOOD, C. RICH, J. N. DANFORTH, R. W. CLARK, T. J. SHEPHERD, J. KNOX, J. F. COOK, W. T. SPROLE, P. H. SNOW, E. BALLENTYNE, J. R. ECKARD, R. A. SMITH, H. MATTHEWS, S. WASHBURNE, W. T. EVA, A. G. CAROTHERS, B. SUNDERLAND, E. J. NEWLIN, T. N. HASKELL, H. DUNNING, W. T. CATTO. Twenty pastoral relations were dissolved, and twenty-three ministers dismissed to other bodies. Eleven Licentiates were ordained; eight candidates for the ministry had been under the care of the Presbytery: R. A. SMITH, C. H. NOURSE, P. H. SNOW, H. MATTHEWS, J. F. COOK, T. J. SHEPHERD, A. G. CAROTHERS, and J. E. NOURSE, the first seven of whom were ordained; the one last named, by the Presbytery of Baltimore.

From the year 1857 to the date of the reunion of the churches the acts of the Presbytery were necessarily few, the agitations of the whole country continuing to exert their influence so largely in this section. Between 1857 and 1862 three ministers, Revs. T. B. McFALLS, J. N. COOMBS, and MOSES JEWELL were received; between the last-named date and 1868, six, Revs. H. H. GARNETT, T. M. McCANN, C. P. GLOVER, W. HART, S. J. MARTIN, J. L. FRENCH. J. G. HAMNER, Jr., W. B. EVANS, and B. F. TANNER, three Licentiates, were received and ordained; between 1862 and 1869, four Licentiates, G. H. SMYTH, D. H. FRAZIER, S. D. NOYES, and J. ROGERS; of whom the first three were ordained.

In the whole period of 1857 to 1869 eleven pastoral relations were constituted, and the same number dissolved. Nine ministers were dismissed to other bodies.

Among the resolutions adopted by the Presbytery in 1865 was the significant one which reads: " *Resolved,* That we look for- " ward with gratitude to Almighty God to the approach of that " day, apparently not far distant, when the institution of slavery " shall cease to exist in all lands, and to that glorious future when

" all men shall be free in that liberty wherein Christ makes His
" people free." Within the trials through which the churches
passed in the last years preceding the reunion, a rich season of
refreshing in spiritual things was graciously experienced. The
Narrative of 1868 said with thankfulness: " The minds of men
" are now assuming the air of calm thoughtfulness; those
" hitherto thoughtless are anxious to place themselves under the
" shield of Him who hath done so wondrously." In the FOURTH
CHURCH, for five months, a revival had progressed, resulting in
the addition of 81.hopeful members to its communion; in other
Churches, also, like seasons had been granted of God. The aggregate number of conversions had swelled the membership of the
Presbytery beyond that of any gathered in a preceding year.

To the close of the war in 1865, the depressed state of the
Churches was such as the troublous times created; it is described
in the paper read by Dr. Sunderland, at the Centennial of Baltimore Presbytery, as a period when its " members were a mere
" handful of men and (until the re-union with the Synod of Phila-
" delphia, in 1863) without any other ecclesiastical fraternity or
" sympathy; moving, as it were, on a bridge of sighs between
" life and death." In their Narrative on the state of religion
made to the Synod in 1863, they said " Owing to our geographical
" position, we have suffered in our spiritual progress by the war.
" The number in our communion is not so large; we live in a
" whirl of commotion. The District is the focus where all the
" troubles of the whole country converge; consequently, our
" youth are led away from serious thought, while the parades,
" the tramp of armies, and the news of battles, almost invariably
" reaching us on the Sabbath, seriously interfere with the effi-
" ciency of preaching."

Some of the Churches, as is well known, were taken possession
of by the Government for Hospitals for the wounded and sick
soldiery. The religion of the Churches was, however, called into
a new field of activity, by the most active testimonies, not only
of their patriotism, but of their charity and good works in the
assiduous physical and spiritual care of the dying and the sick.

Such was the doubtful outlook at the close of the year 1868,
when movements were inaugurated for the reunion of the Church
at large. For this the vote of the Presbytery, with a single excep-

tion, was a hearty " Aye." It had fulfilled a mission of widely extended usefulness. To the roll of the six Churches of which it consisted at its organization in 1823 had been added, as has been shown, the F STREET CHURCH in 1824, and by organization, the FOURTH CHURCH, Washington, in 1829 ; the SYKESVILLE, 1839 ; the FIFTEENTH, Washington, and FIFTH and the SIXTH, Baltimore, in 1842 ; the SHARON, at Tenallytown, and the MIDDLEBROOK and POOLESVILLE, in Maryland, in 1847 ; the QUARRIES in the same State in 1848 ; the ASSEMBLY'S and SIXTH CHURCH, Washington, and the GREEN STREET, Baltimore, in 1853; the WESTERN CHURCH, Washington, in 1855; in all, fourteen. Of these the SIXTH, Baltimore, and the SHARON died out. The FIFTH, Baltimore, and SECOND, Washington, were dropped from the roll by their leaving the Presbytery. Under its care had been built the FOURTH FIFTEENTH, ASSEMBLY'S, SIXTH, and WESTERN in Washington, and, by its aid, largely those in the adjacent country.

Of the Ministers who were the first members at its organization, Rev. Professor MAFFIT had died in 1828, Dr. BALCH in 1833, BRECKENRIDGE in 1844, MINES in 1849, BAKER in 1857, POST in 1858, HARRISON in 1863, and CAMPBELL in 1864 ; to whose names must be added in memoriam, also, those of S. WASHBURNE, Moderator, in 1853 ; Rev. THOMAS L. HAMNER, the successful worker in the Sabbath-School cause, 1854 ; Rev. JOHN F. COOK, teacher and Pastor of the FIFTEENTH STREET CHURCH (colored), 1855 ; Rev. JOSHUA DANFORTH, successively Pastor of the FOURTH CHURCH, Washington, and of the SECOND CHURCH, Alexandria, 1862 ; Rev. A. G. CAROTHERS, Pastor of the ASSEMBLY'S CHURCH at its organization, who died in the West Indies in the vain search for renewed health, 1863 ; Rev. MOSES JEWELL, 1864 ; Rev. A. D. HOLLISTER, 1865 ; Rev. H. DUNNING, 1869.

II. The Presbytery of Potomac.—1858-1870.

In 1858 the Old School Churches in Washington and its vicinity were feeling more and more the pressing need of a new organization to have more immediate and local care of their interests and those of the neighboring counties in Maryland and Virginia, where they desired to extend their efforts. The Synod of Baltimore cordially created the Presbytery of Potomac, thus separating from it the ministers who, with their Churches, had been merged, as has been shown, in that of Baltimore for the previous four years.

The order of the Synod was that the Ministers composing the new Presbytery and its congregations should be those of the Baltimore body within the territory bounded by a line from the mouth of the Potomac, and with it to the northern boundary of. Montgomery county, Maryland; thence along the northern and Eastern boundaries of that and of Anne Arundel counties to Elkridge landing; thence to the mouth of the Severn; and thence along Chesapeake Bay to the point of beginning. The Presbytery thus constituted consisted of Ministers, J. J. GRAEE, P. D. GURLEY, S. TUSTIN, J. E. NOURSE, D. MOTZER, J. H. BOCOCK, B. F. BITTINGER, and J. E. WALTON—with the churches of F STREET, the SECOND, and SEVENTH, Washington; BRIDGE STREET, Georgetown; ANNAPOLIS, NEELSVILLE, DARNESTOWN, BLADENSBURG, and WEST RIVER in Maryland. A small beginning; only eight ministers, several of them without pastoral charge, and only two churches of financial or numerical strength.

The Presbytery was not disheartened. At its first meeting, November 30th of the same year, its two earliest acts were the appointment of a Committee on assessments, and the adoption of a resolution that every minister should spend, in the intervals of the stated meetings, at least one Sabbath in missionary labor.

The earliest result of this last named act was the revival and continuance of Presbyterian services at Laurel, Maryland.

The next year, the Synod transferred to the Presbytery that part of the territory of Winchester Presbytery comprising the counties of Alexandria, Fairfax, Loudoun, Prince William, Stafford, Fauquier, King George, Westmoreland, Richmond, Northumberland and Lancaster; thus adding the following ten Ministers: T. B. BALCH, E. HARRISON, C. B. MCKEE, R. S. BELL, E. B. SMITH, A. M. HERSHEY, J. W. PUGH, A. D. POLLOCK, T. S. WITHEROW and J. B. DAVIS; with the Churches of FIRST ALEXANDRIA, FIRST PRINCE WILLIAM, LEWINSVILLE, GREENWICH, WARRENTON, YELLOW CHAPEL, RAPPAHANNOCK, SALEM, and LOVETTSVILLE, in Virginia, and BETHESDA, in Maryland. In the same year, the union of the F STREET and the SECOND CHURCH, Washington, into the NEW YORK AVENUE CHURCH, largely increased the influence of Presbyterianism in the national Capital, and by the wealth, activity and missionary spirit of this new organization extended the efforts of the Presbytery in its missionary work.

The rapidly growing excitement of the slavery question, however, and its culmination in the approaching contest between the North and the South, for a time arrested all possible further church extension, and brought the loss of the territory transferred by the Synod in 1859.

The Minutes of the Presbytery of September, 1861, record that at that appointed day for the meeting of the Presbytery two ministers only, Revs. Dr. GURLEY and BITTINGER, were present to respond to the roll call; and two Churches only were represented by Elders. It was afterwards learned that the members of the body residing in Virginia held a meeting on the same day at Greenwich, to which the Presbytery had adjourned from its previous meeting.

These Ministers claimed that theirs was the true body. The Synod decided that, under the circumstances, the suspension of all intercourse between the District and Virginia by the begun hostilities, the meeting in Washington was justified, and the true Presbytery had met there; but all questions as to this were virtually settled by the continued separation of the two sections of country and by the war.

Very soon after the happy cessation of the civil contest, the loss of the Virginia territory was repaired. New activities were aroused. In 1864, the present METROPOLITAN CHURCH effort was begun, even under the war-cloud shadows, and its organization of a church of rapidly increasing promise, effected first under the name of the CAPITOL HILL CHURCH, April 11th of that year.

The North Church organization followed in 1865. In Maryland, under Rev. J. S. H. Henderson, the Church at Darnestown was revived. In Fairfax county, Virginia, Rev. H. P. Dechert gathered back the congregation at the historic Church of Lewinsville, and effected an organization at Falls Church. In Prince William county, under Rev. J. E. Nourse, the First Prince William Church was restord, regular services held, and a new organization and house of worship secured at Manassas. The rolls of the Churches in 1866 showed an increase of membership from 679 in 1859 to 1,272.

The position of the Presbytery in relation to the national struggle had not been without true and unmistakable deliverance.

In May, 1862, resolutions introduced by Rev. Dr. Tustin were unanimously passed, affirming, in substance, that all wise and good Governments are the product of the power and wisdom of God ; that the Government of the United States is eminently the off-spring of His abounding grace; that, in the opinion of the Presbytery, the uprising of the people who desired to overturn it was an act of wrong and folly ; that it heartily approved the measures of the President taken to preserve unimpaired the legacy of our fathers ; and that its deepest gratitude was due to the Great Ruler of Nations for His guidance and protection during the contest, for which the Presbytery would continue ever to pray until the return of peace should bring again a united and happy people.

During the years 1859 to 1870 were added to the eight ministers who had formed the Presbytery in 1858 : April 25, 1859, Rev. E. Bosworth, from the Presbytery of Baltimore ; 1862, May 8, Rev. F. T. Brown, from that of Western Reserve, and W. Y. Brown, from that of Carlisle; October 12th, J. S. H. Henderson, from the same ; 13th, H. Snyder, from that of Roanoke ; in 1864, April 11th, Rev. J. Chester, from the Presbytery of Burlington ; November 4th, W. W. Campbell, from that of West Virginia; in 1865, April 11, J. R. Fisher, from that of Buffalo; May 1st, G. H. Hair, from that of White Water ; June 16th, A. A. E. Taylor, from that of Dubuque; October 4th, W. B. Evans, from that of the District of Columbia ; December 5th, L. R. Fox, from that of Burlington ; in 1866, April

5th, S. J. Baird and W. T. VanDoren, from the Presbytery of West Jersey and from the Classis of Michigan; September 13th, G. H. McCampbell, from the Presbytery of New Albany; in 1867 (J. E. Nourse and B. F. Bittinger, who had been for a time under the Presbytery of Baltimore); in 1868, T. G. Murphey, from that of Lewes; in 1869, S. S. Mitchell, from that of Carlisle; in 1870, February 25th, D. W. Moffat, from the Presbytery of Madison. Thirteen Ministers had been dismissed to other bodies.

In April, 1870, the total membership of the Churches of the Presbytery was but 1,094. The losses had occurred by removals, deaths, and the revision of the rolls. In the Narrative on the state of religion of that year the report to the Synod said the Presbytery looked with earnest hope that, in the additional strength of the contemplated reunion, it would be permitted to accomplish more for the glory of the Redeemer. Its final meeting was held June 9, 1870. For the reunion of the two bodies it had been for some time heartily desirous. In 1863 it had made overtures for this in the way of uniting with the District Presbytery in missionary work; in the year following it passed a resolution favoring reunion. Its most influential pastor, Rev. Dr. Gurley, was one of the Committee conferring on it with that appointed by New School Assembly of 1868. The consolidation into the Washington City Presbytery made June 30th was cordially accepted. The two were made one in Christian fellowship and labor.

2

III. The Presbytery of Washington City.--1870-1888.

The period of about thirty-three years during which the two Presbyteries had been virtually separated had been one of momentous interest in both church and state. The influence of the excitements of the war at home and of the political changes abroad marked itself notably on all branches of the Church here ; especially did the wide openings for the spread of the gospel and the spirit of union and communion, freshly awakened among Christians, betoken a day of promise. These influences received within the Presbyteries a further and grateful impulse arising from the salvation of the Government and the reunion of the States. The times were ripe for the consolidation of which mention has been made.

The organization of the united body as ordered by the Synod of Baltimore under the direction of the United General Assembly of May, 1870, was effected in the BRIDGE STREET CHURCH, June 20th of the year, the opening prayer being offered by DR. S. TUSTIN, the oldest ordained Minister present, and the Moderator elected being DR. J. C. SMITH. The first Stated Clerk was REV. T. B. McFALLS.

The Ministers enrolled in the order of their ordinations were DRS. S. TUSTIN, J. C. SMITH, T. W. SIMPSON and W. MoLAIN ; REVS. W. T. VANDOREN and J. S. H. HENDERSON ; DRS. BYRON SUNDERLAND and B. F. BITTINGER, REVS. T. G. MURPHY, J. N. COOMBS, J. E. NOURSE ; REV. T. B. McFALLS, DR. J. CHESTER, D. W. MOFFAT, J. L. FRENCH, W. HART, L. R. FOX and S. S. MITCHELL.

The following-named Churches were enrolled : BLADENSBURG (now HYATTSVILLE), BRIDGE STREET (now WEST STREET), NEW YORK AVENUE, FIRST, FOURTH, FIFTEENTH ST., SIXTH, ASSEMBLY'S, SEVENTH (now WESTMINSTER), WESTERN, METROPOLITAN, and NORTH CHURCHES, WASHINGTON ; FIRST PRINCE WILLIAM, MANASSAS and CLIFTON and the Churches among the Freedmen in Virginia ; NEELSVILLE and DARNESTOWN, Montgomery county, Md.

At the date of this reunion of the Presbyteries, their total membership reported to the General Assembly was 2,893, viz :

of the District body, 1,799; of the Potomac, 1,094. The number of the Churches (including those among the freedmen under the District Presbytery) was about equal. These totals may be taken as a standpoint from which the present state of the united body may be considered.

The meetings during the next five years were frequent, and the roll of the Presbytery much enlarged. Within the decade, to 1880, were received from other Presbyteries and by ordinations, the ministers whose names here follow: In 1870, from the Methodist Episcopal Church, Rev. L. Dobson; from the Presbytery of Cincinnati, Dr. C. B. Boynton; and from that of Iowa City, Rev. A. Fairley; in 1871, from the Presbytery of New Brunswick, Rev. C. R. Von Romondt; from that of Brooklyn, New York, Rev. Mason Noble; from Newcastle Presbytery, Rev. C. Beach; from the Congregational Association of Dubuque, W. H. Rice; from the Presbytery of Morris and Orange, W. Bradley; and by ordination, D. H Riddle and W. McAttee: in 1872, from the Presbytery of Holston, Tennessee, Rev. J. G. Mason; and by ordination, W. H. Logan: in 1873, from the Presbytery of Binghampton, N. Y., Dr. S. H. Howe; from that of Sacramento, California, J. Brown; from that of Whitewater, Indiana, Rev. G. O. Little; from that of Chester, Pennsylvania, Rev. L. Westcott: in 1874, from the Presbytery of Chesapeake, Rev. C. H. Nourse; from that of Utica, Rev. G. Van Deurs; and by ordination, Rev. J. T. Kelly: in 1875, from the Presbytery of Niagara, N. Y., Rev. J. Odell; from that of New York, Rev. H. P. Dechert; from that of Marion, Georgia, Dr. D. Wills; from that of Buffalo, Rev. P. H. Burghardt; and by ordination, J. A. Carmichael, G. B. Patch, and C. B. Ramsdell: in 1876, from the Presbytery of Otsego, N. Y., Rev. S. Murdock: in 1877, from that of Cleveland, Ohio, Rev. N. Cobb; and from that of Saginaw, Michigan, Rev. A. McSween: in 1878, Revs. C. W. Landau, from the Presbytery of Hudson, New York; T. S. Wynkoop, from that of Allahabad, Indiana; Rev. J. R. Paxton, from that of Carlisle, Pennsylvania; and by ordination, F. I. Grimke, F. M. Todd, and A. J. Henry.

Within the years of the present decade have been received from the Presbytery of New York, Rev. J. G. Craighead, in 1880; in 1881, Rev. C. Noble, from the Congregational Association of Washington City; E. H. CUMPSTON, from the Presbytery of Winchester; A. POULSON, from that of Philadelphia Central; and C. HERR, L. MILLER, and H. UNGLAUB, by ordination; in 1882, Revs. S. S. WALLEN, from the Presbytery of Huntington, Pennsylvania; Drs. W. A. BARTLETT and J. DUDLEY, from that of Indianapolis; Dr. C. H. A. BUCKLEY, from that of Champlain, New York; in 1883, Dr. T. S. CHILDS, from the Presbytery of Westchester, N. Y.; J. M. NOURSE, from that of Athens, Ohio; and by ordination, H. CLARKE; in 1884, Dr. T. FULLERTON, from the Presbytery of Erie, Pennsylvania; W. J. MCILVAIN, from that of Baltimore; E. PECK, from that of Otsego, N. Y.; and by ordination, F. M. BURDICK; in 1885, C. H. RAYMOND, from the Presbytery of Indianapolis, and D. L. RATHBUN, from that of Baltimore; in 1886, Dr. T. S. HAMLIN, from that of Cincinnati; W. H. Edwards, from that of Newcastle, and G. P. VAN WYCK, from that of Topeka, Kansas; in 1887, J. R. RILEY, from that of Louisville, Kentucky; R. H. FLEMING, from that of Winchester; M. P. SNELL, from the Congregational Association of Washington City; S. F. HERSHEY, from the Presbytery of Dayton; and by ordination, MARTIN HOLMES. The whole number has been thus 63.

Since the organization of the Presbytery have been dismissed to other bodies: In 1870, Rev. J. H. BECKWITH, W. Hart, and W. STRYKER; in 1871, L. R. FOX; in 1872, Dr. D. W. Moffat; in 1873, W. H. RHOBERTS and W. B. WALLER; in 1874, B. A. WILLIAMSON, L. DOBSON, and W. H. LOGAN; in 1875, W. A. MCATTEE and Dr. C. B. BOYNTON; in 1876, W. H. RICE and W. D. ROBERTS; in 1877, J. G. MASON, J. A. CARMICHAEL, and J. BROWN; in 1878, J. R. HENDERSON, L. R. JOHNSON, and Dr. S. S. MITCHELL; in 1879, F. CLENDENIN, W. E. CARR; in 1880, S. M. BEACH and G. T. JENNINGS; in 1881, S. MURDOCK, W. EMERY, and C. NOBLE; in 1882, E. WARREN, J. R. PAXTON, C. JOELL, H. N. BROWN, and A. G. DAVIS; in 1883, H. UNGLAUB, C. HERR, C. DILLARD, and S. H. HOWE; in 1884, D. WILLS, Jr., C. R. VON ROMONDT, H. CLARKE; in 1885, S. S. WALLEN and F. J. GRIMKE; in 1886, R. D. HARLAN, S. S. WALLEN, and E. A. LOWE; in 1887, W. CHESTER, Dr. D. WILLS, R. H. FLEMING, and J. P. FOSTER. Of these, 14 only were Pastors or Stated Supplies, the remainder being either Licentiates or candidates for the Ministry.

The following Churches have been organized: Clifton, Va., 1870, GURLEY MISSION, Washington, 1871; FALLS CHURCH, Virginia, February 3, 1873; VIENNA, Virginia, November 16, 1873; HERMON, Maryland, January 5, 1874; EASTERN, Washington City, D. C., May 19, 1875; BOYD's STATION, Maryland, May 13, 1877; ZION EVANGELICAL, Washington City, D. C.; OAK GROVE, Virginia, September 25th, 1881; UNITY, Washington City, D. C., April 15, 1882; MOUNT HERMON, Virginia, September 3, 1882; and CHURCH OF THE COVENANT, Washington City, D. C., October 13, 1885.

Between the dates of June 20, 1870, and the close of the year 1887, the following installations were made: In 1870, October 6th, REV. C. B. BOYNTON over the ASSEMBLY's CHURCH, 6th street; in 1871, April 25th, REV. D. H. RIDDLE, FALLS CHURCH, Virginia; May 10th, W. A. McATEE, FIRST ALEXANDRIA; October 30th, C. BEACH, DARNESTOWN, Maryland; in 1872, October 8th, J. G.MASON, NORTH CHURCH; in 1873, June 9th, G. LITTLE, ASSEMBLY CHURCH, and J. BROWN, LEWINSVILLE, Fairfax county, Virginia; in 1874, May 4th, J. T. KELLY, FOURTH CHURCH; May 10th, G. VANDEURS, 15TH ST. CHURCH; in 1875, May 9th, DR. D. WILLS, WESTERN CHURCH; June 18th, J. ODELL, LEWINSVILLE, Fairfax county, Virginia; June 20th, J. BROWN, 15TH STREET; November 1st, G. B. PATCH, EASTERN CHURCH; December 13th, C. B. RAMSDELL, NORTH CHURCH; in 1878, June 11th, G. W. LANDAU, ZION EVANGELICAL; July 7th, F. J. GRIMKE, 15TH STREET CHURCH; October 23d, T. S. WYNKOOP, WESTERN CHURCH; October 27th, F. M. TODD, MANASSAS, Prince William county, Virginia; November 10th, J. R. PAXTON, N. Y. AVENUE; in 1879, June 8th, S. H. HOWE, WEST STREET, Georgetown; in 1881, October 17th, H. UNGLAUB, ZION EVANGELICAL; in 1882, April 10th, S. S. WALLEN, EASTERN CHURCH; April 19th, G. B. PATCH, UNITY CHURCH; October 24th, W. A. BARTLETT, N. Y. AVENUE; in 1883, April 24th, H. CLARK, LEWINSVILLE and VIENNA; November 14th, J. M. NOURSE, DARNESTOWN CHURCH, Montgomery county, Maryland; in 1884, February 13th, E. PECK, EASTERN CHURCH; April 23d, F. H. BURDICK, 6TH CHURCH; in 1885, October 15th, W. J. McILVAIN, HYATTSVILLE CHURCH, Prince George county, Maryland; October 28th, D. L. RATHBUN, DARNESTOWN, Maryland; November 4th,

Dr. T. Fullerton, West Street, Georgetown; in 1886, October 12th, W. H. Edwards, Lewinsville and Vienna; November 9th, Dr. T. S. Hamlin, Church of the Covenant; in 1887, January 18th, J. R. Riley, 15th Street; October 18th, S. F. Hershey, 6th Church.

In all 35 pastoral relations were constituted, of which to the date of December 27, 1887, twenty have been dissolved; a large number, but accounted for chiefly by the fluctuating character of the resident population of the city, so many of our Church members being in the employ of the changing Government offices, and thus preventing the desired permanence of our Cong regations.

Since the organization of the Presbytery the following Ministers have died: Dr. John C. Smith, January 23, 1878, at the age of 78; Dr. Septimus Tustin, October 28, 1871, aged 67; R. R. Gurley, July 30, 1872, aged 75; Dr. William McClain, 1873, aged 68; T. B. McFalls, May 22, 1873, aged 38; John N. Coombs, December 27, 1874, aged 58; Charles H. Nourse, July 14, 1876, aged 58; T. C. Murphy, January 9, 1878, aged 61; Lorenzo Westcott, June 5, 1878, aged 50; Mason Noble, October 24, 1881, aged 72; James S. H. Henderson, August 17, 1882, aged 67; E. H. Cumpston, January 1, 1885, aged 71; William T. Vandoren, December 20, 1885, aged 66; P. H. Burghardt, July 22, 1886, aged 75; C. H. Raymond, October 30, 1886, aged 68; and the following, the dates of whose deaths and ages have not been available for record: Rev. H. P. Dechert, Ward Batchelor, and C. M. Parks. In all 18.

The goodly age to which nearly all of these were spared for the work of the Kingdom will be observed, and it is their record that all were employed in this to the close of life. The distressing circumstances of the mental aberration causing the decease of Rev. J. N. Coombs are well known.

During the eighteen years of the Presbytery, the number of its ministers increased from 19 to 35; of Communicants from 2,839 to 4,776; of Sabbath-School membership from 3,124 to 6,153; of contributions to benevolent objects from $6,445 to $12,799; of sums reported under the head of " Congregational " from $50,190 to $119,226. The Presbytery now consists of 34 Ministers, and has under its care 32 Churches, connected with which are 4,776 Communicants; 118 Ruling Elders; 55 Deacons; 4 Licentiates, and 14 Candidates for the gospel ministry.

If from the roll of the thirty-two Churches reported to the Synod of 1887, those are excepted which have never settled a pastor, viz., NEELSVILLE and its outgrowth BOYD'S STATION, and HERMON in Maryland; and FIRST PRINCE WILLIAM and CLIFTON, Virginia; and if further exception be made of those among the Freedmen in Amelia County, Virginia, of which Churches no definite accounts have been found available, the efficient strength of the Presbytery is more correctly considered as that of twenty-one pastoral relations. Nine Ministers are without charge, though frequently in service.

During the period of 1870 to 1888 a proper zeal for the Sanctuary has prompted the erection of ten church edifices, viz.: METROPOLITAN, WEST STREET, EASTERN, UNITY, and CHURCH OF THE COVENANT, WASHINGTON; and MANASSAS, VIENNA, CLIFTON, BOYD STATION, HERMON, and FALLS CHURCH, in the adjacent counties. It has also prompted the enlargement or beautifying of an equal number, viz., those of the NEW YORK AVENUE, FOURTH CHURCH, WESTMINSTER, NORTH, WESTERN, METROPOLITAN, WEST STREET, WASHINGTON; and LEWINSVILLE, HYATTSVILLE and CLIFTON.

· A proper account of the benevolent work of the Churches under the care of the Presbytery includes the contributions of the Women's Societies to this object. By the kindness of Mrs. M. A. Boyd, Treasurer of the Women's Society for Home Missions, the statement is recorded that " The first money received from " the Women of Washington City Presbytery came from the " FIRST CHURCH June 26th, 1879, and the sums for the years fol- " lowing were as follows: In 1879 to 1880, $534; 1880 to 1881, " $620.69; 1881 to 1882, $594.95; 1882 to 1883, $703.86; 1883 " to 1884, $1,098.10; 1884 to 1885, $1,543.47; 1885 to 1886, $2,- " 246,36; 1886 to 1887, $2,362.47; 1887 to January 1st, 1888, " $1,101.94—or in all, to the close of the third quarter of the " year 1887, $10,805.84.

By the kindness of Mrs. Julia M. Fishburne, Treasurer of the Woman's Foreign Missionary Society, has also been received the following account of the contributions to that object, viz:

" So far as I can learn the first receipt from Washington was " in 1875, $500.00; in 1876, $400.00; in 1877, $500.00. This

" brings it to the organization of the Presbyterian Society, 1878–
" 1879. The sums received since that date have been for the
" year ending May, 1879, $179.00; 1880, $1,103.26; 1881,
" $1,067.56; 1882, $761.22; 1883, $1,169.63; 1884, $983.87;
" 1885, $1,332.76; 1886, $1,196.99; 1887, $1,882.53; or in all,
" from 1879 to January 1, 1887, $9,876.72.

In the Minutes of the Synod of Baltimore, of 1887, will be found in the Report of the Synod's Women's Committee on Home Missions, the statement for Home Missions, that " Gifts " from the Washington City Presbytery had amounted to " $2,383.66, and in boxes to $662.30. There are 22 Auxiliaries " and 8 Bands out of the 32 Churches, six of the remaining " churches being among the Freedmen, and under the Freed- " men's Board. There are but four where further organizations " may be looked for. "

In the same Minutes will also be found the statement as to. Women's Work for Foreign Missions, that the receipts for the year ending March, 1887, were $2,103.63. The Committee of the Synod in their report on the state of religion for the same year, speak of " the decided increase in both the numbers and the gifts received by these two societies."

The Presbytery has, for some years, maintained a deep interest in the instructions received by the young men at the Howard University. Two of our members, Rev. CHARLES H. A. BUCKLEY, D.D., and Rev. J. G. CRAIGHEAD, D.D., hold chairs as professors in the University. To its funds our Churches also contribute. A number of its graduates are in the ministry of our Churches.

This imperfect Memorial of the Presbytery may prompt in the minds and hearts of its readers the reflections, among others, that, although an extended and useful work has been carried on, " much lands remain to be possessed." The rapidly advancing population of this great city assuredly calls for greater corresponding Church extension by all our Evangelical denominations. The Association recently formed under the auspices of the Presbytery embraces within it much of promise for this end.

The number of Ministers enrolled in the several Presbyteries herein named reaches closely the figures 140. Of these, a large majority have been candidates or Licentiates, who have located beyond our bounds. A large majority have passed to their reward on high. The attention of Pastors and of Christian parents may be invoked for an increase in the number of the baptized children of the Covenant to be consecrated from their youth to the Ministry. The Societies forming in the several Churches among our young people are a happy token of good for this.

OFFICERS OF THE PRESBYTERY.—Moderator, Tennis S. Hamlin, D. D.; Stated Clerk, B. F. Bittinger, D. D.

HOME MISSIONS.—T. S. Childs, D. D., Rev. J. E. Nourse, B. F. Bittinger, D. D., John Chester, D. D.; Ruling Elders: Wm. Ballantyne, C. H. Carrington.

FOREIGN MISSIONS.—Rev. J. W. McIlvain, Rev. T. S. Wynkoop, Rev. J. Dudley; R. E.: W. H. H. Warman.

CHURCH ERECTION.—Rev. George O. Little, Rev. D. Riddle, Rev. D. S. Rathbun; R. E.: J. H. Meriwether.

PUBLICATION AND S. SCHOOL WORK.—Rev. J. M. Nourse, Rev. E. Peck; R. E.: T. Swazey.

EDUCATION.—Rev. G. B. Patch, Rev. J. M. Nourse; R. E.: S. L. Crissey.

FREEDMEN.—T. S. Hamlin, D. D., W. A. Bartlett, D. D.; R. E.: Commodore J. W. Easby.

MINISTERIAL RELIEF.—Rev. J. T. Kelly, Rev. F. M. Todd, Rev. S. F. Hershey, Ph. D.; R. E.: C. B. Church.

AID TO COLLEGES AND ACADEMIES.—J G. Craighead, D. D., B. Sunderland, D. D.; R. E.: W. H. H. Smith.

TEMPERANCE.—Rev. C. B. Ramsdell, Rev. J. W. McIlvain, T. S. Hamlin, D. D.; R. E.: T. B. Dalrymple.

SYSTEMATIC BENEFICENCE.—Rev. T. S. Wynkoop, Rev. J. L. French; R. E.: Charles Lyman.

SABBATH SCHOOLS.—Rev. J. M. Nourse, Rev. G. P. VanWyck; R. E.: D. McFarlan.

THEOLOGY.—T. Fullerton, D. D., B. F. Bittinger, D. D.

CHURCH HISTORY.—B. Sunderland, D. D., J. Chester, D. D.

CHURCH GOVERNMENT AND SACRAMENTS.—T. S. Childs, D. D., Rev. N. Cobb, Rev. W. H. Edwards.

HEBREW.—Rev. J. W. McIlvain, Rev. T. S. Wynkoop.

GREEK.—J. Chester, D. D., Rev. Alexander Fairley.

Bladensburg Church, Prince George County, Md. 1718; now Hyattsville Church.

This church, six miles distant from the Capital, is the second in the line of succession to the OLD PATUXENT or UPPER MARLBOROUH CHURCH, which existed before the close of the last century, and was represented in 1704 in the Synod of Philadelphia by Rev. NATHANIEL TAYLOR. The intermediate link was the OLD BLADENSBURG, organized in 1718, by Rev. HUGH CONN, minister from Scotland. Mr. CONN appears to have remained with the Church until his sudden death in the pulpit in 1752. Of the MARLBOROUGH CHURCH Mr. NINIAN BEALL was a liberal friend, donating the grounds for the building, and, most probably, also the communion service—one of old English plate of the date of 1707, which, at the closing of the MARLBOROUGH CHURCH, was sent to Bladensburg. The Hyattsville Communion still holds that portion of it which has been preserved.

At the formation of the Presbytery of Baltimore in 1786, Bladensburg was represented by Rev. JAMES HUNT, from whose death, in 1793, the Church had either stated supplies or the short pastoral relations of Rev. Messrs. SEMPLE, KNOX, MAFFIT, WILLEY, and VEITCH—until the appointment under the General Assembly in 1809, of Rev. J. BRECKENRIDGE to labor here and at Washington City. Mr. Breckenridge remained with the Church three years, and, after the short pastorate of Rev. T. C. Searle, returned and again served the Church from 1823 to 1830. The roll of communicants at that date numbered 71, and the attendance on the pulpit ministrations was full.

From this time until 1858, with the exception of the short pastorate of Rev. John Decker (1843–'44), the Church again had the service only of stated supplies, chiefly those by Revs. Bosworth, Nevius, Crawford, Baird, French and Simpson—by the last named from 1851 to 1858. It was then attached to the Presbytery of Potomac. In 1867, it connected itself with the Patapsco Presbytery of the Church South, and was for three years under the care of Rev. John Ross until the organization of the Washington City Presbytery.

Hyattsville Church.

The village of Bladensburg had been for long years on the decline. The congregation had become very small and the building itself, rebuilt as far back as 1818, was uninviting. In 1873, by the efforts largely of the late W. P. Shedd and his family, a new enterprise in the adjacent and growing village of Hyattsville was begun in prayer and faith. Mr. Shedd, a member of the Fourth Church, Washington, had removed to Bladensburg a few years before, and was earnestly alive to the need of a Presbyterian Church in the village. With the encouragement of the Washington City Presbytery, seconded by the Pastors of the New York Avenue, First Presbyterian, Westminster, Metropolitan, and Sixth Churches, a revival of the old Presbyterian interest was secured, and the corner-stone of a new building laid October 24, 1874. The house was dedicated in 1876; the new name of the Church having been authorized by the act of the Presbytery. The old building of 1818 was disposed of to the Baptist Congregation for the sum of 800 dollars. From this time until the call of the present Pastor, the pulpit was supplied chiefly by Rev. Dr. Simpson, followed by Messrs. Chickering, Burghardt, and Lowe.

The present Pastor, Rev. J. W. McIlvain; was intalled October 12, 1885. The prospects of this Church are very encouraging. The surrounding population is on the advance. Recent improvements made to the building have increased its value to that of $5,000, and a neat Manse of an additional value of $3,000 has been donated by Mr. J. J. Shedd, a brother of the founder, under God, of the New Church. The roll of communicants numbers 42; of the S. School, 84.

The columns for the agencies of the Church reported to the Assembly are well filled. The Church this year becomes self-sustaining.

Officers.—*Pastor*, Rev. William J. McIlvain ·, *Elders*, F. H. Smith, F. E. Baukhages, S. A. Holton.

The earliest records of this Church take us back to the days of the jealous watchfulness of all Churches other than the Church of England, as the only true one for the colonies. In 1760, the Presbyterians of the city received a license from the Governor and Council of Virginia to worship according to their order, said license requiring them to "keep the Church building doors and entrance unlocked," lest something obnoxious to the Royal power might be concocted therein. After worshipping for some time under this permit in the Town Hall, they built a house from the earnings of a lottery, an act, in its judgment of its rightfulness, not confined to these Christians, but to be found in the records of other sections of the country, as in accordance with the ideas of the times. In the present building is a tablet bearing the inscription, "Organized 1772; Church erected 1774." The ground was deeded "to Rev. WILLIAM THOM, the first Pastor, and to his successors, who shall be Presbyterian Ministers, elected and appointed to officiate in the Presbyterian Church," the building "to be kept solely for the use of said Church;" a provision restraining its sale, for any removal to a better location, unless by later and special legislation.

Mr. THOM was buried alongside of his Church, and was succeeded in 1786 by Rev. ISAAC S. KEITH; and he, by REV. JAMES MUIR, whose pastorate extended from 1789 to 1820. A marble tablet commemorates his faithful labors.

Dr. ELIAS HARRISON's ministry followed, extending from the death of Dr. MUIR, to his death, February 13, 1863. Three years before his election as Pastor, a secession had resulted in the organization of the Second Church; and in the latter part of his Pastorate (1861) the congregation became divided by the war, the majority remaining loyal to this day, to the Northern Assembly. Dr. HARRISON was a faithful and revered Pastor.

The temporary supply of the pulpit by Rev. Mr. AXTEL and others followed; two Pastors, Rev. G. M. McCAMPBELL and W. A. McATEE being next successively in charge until 1874; after which the building was leased until 1880, to about 100 persons, who seceded from the 2D CHURCH and formed the "UNION

CHURCH," under Rev. Dr. BULLOCK; two of the elders, and nearly all of the members of the 2d Church uniting also with these. From the date of the dissolution of this organization, the pulpit was supplied by members of the Washington City Presbytery, and very frequently by Rev. Mr. E. Whittelsey, of the Congregational Church. In May, 1885, Rev. James Nourse was installed by the Presbytery of Washington City.

It thus appears from the Church records that its Pastors have been successively in connection with the several Presbyteries of Donegal, Pennsylvania, 1st Philadelphia, Baltimore, the District of Columbia, Potomac, and Washington. In 1808 the General Assembly was invited to hold its sessions in this Church; the Assembly, however, continued to meet in Philadelphia—1800 to 1835.

The congregation have frequently labored under peculiar difficulties. It is believed that the secession of 1817 would not have occurred had that eminent evangelist, Rev. Sylvester Larned, or the equally zealous Pastor, Daniel Baker, accepted a call to become co-pastor with the venerable Dr. Muir, in his declining health. The division resulted, however, in the formation of a second and prosperous Church. July 20, 1835, the FIRST CHURCH edifice was destroyed by lightning at the hour of expected service, and for the two following years the congregation worshipped with the SECOND CHURCH. At a later date the more serious embarrassments which have been referred to have continned to dishearten friends, who, by the memories of the good old times of their fathers and a desire to perpetuate the work to which they have fallen heirs, would gladly see a steady and healthful progress. It is hoped that a new era will dawn.

The sitting capacity of the house is 600; the number of communicants reported to the Assembly of 1887, is 80; an increase of 51 over that of 1879. The columns for contributions to the Board of Assembly are all filled.

OFFICERS.—*Pastor*, Rev. JAMES NOURSE; *Elders*, J. P. AGNEW, N. W. PIERSON; *Trustees*, J. P. AGNEW, PAUL AGNEW, LEWIS McKENZIE.

The First Presbyterian Preaching in the Present District of Columbia.

The first offers of the gospel by our Church in this immediate region date in the year 1780. In March of that year Rev. STEPHEN BLOOMER BALCH, a native of Maryland and a licentiate of the old Donegal Presbytery of Pennsylvania, when on his way to make a missionary tour in the Carolinas, preached to a few persons in Georgetown of Scotch and New England descent—some from that true Scotch Presbyterian, Col. Niman Beall, who had, at a still earlier date, liberally befriended the OLD MARL BOROUGH CHURCH, in Maryland. Mr. BALCH was at once invited to gather a congregation among this people. Returning from North Carolina in the same year, he found an unpromising field, the population of that day being largely of the ruder elements; but he began his labors on the skirts of the neighboring woods, and, under his commission as Evangelist, organized a Church.

His first small congregation, after worshipping for two years in a rented room on the present site of the PRESBYTERIAN MISSION CHAPEL, on Market street, built a very humble house of worship, 30 feet square, at the corner of Washington and Bridge streets. His first elder was a Mr. Orme, son of one of the pastors of the MARLBOROUGH CHURCH; and, at his first service, seven persons only sat down at the communion table, some of the lookers-on, as tradition reports, staring with amazement, having never heard of our Great Atoning Sacrifice. The return of peace from our revolutionary struggle contributed to the growth of the town, which, at the head of the navigation of the day, had a future of promise. Mr. BALCH's congregation grew with it, his eminently catholic spirit attracting members of other denominations until they built their own churches. The location of the first Presbyterian building was fitly chosen to accommodate the people, who then mostly resided below the present Bridge or M street, but also for those living east of Rock creek, within the beginnings of " the Federal City." Among the contributors to its erection were Vice-President Jefferson, then residing in a dwelling which still stands on " Jefferson street," and Secretary Gallatin.

After the establishment of the Government here, members of the Episcopal Church built their house of worship in Washington, but the vacancies in Dr. BALCH's Church were speedily more than filled, and the Church grew in strength. In 1821, the old building was replaced by one of much larger dimensions. Its dismantling was made the occasion of an impressive discourse, reminding the people of God's signal favor to them through the forty years of the past. It is not an uninteresting fact that Dr. BALCH and his successors, down to the times of the late war, provided, with the full co-operation of their people, for Sabbath-School instruction of the colored race.

Dr. BALCH's personal sacrifices during his life were not few. Among them were, in 1831, the destruction of his whole household effects by fire, himself and his wife barely escaping with their lives. The early Sessional Records of the Church were also destroyed, together with a valuable portrait of Makemie.

His ministerial labors were closed in his eighty-seventh year by the call of the Master, on the morning of September 7, 1833, to the rewards of fifty-three years of duty and godly example. In testimony of his worth, the Aldermen and Common Council attended the funeral in a body and the streets were draped in mourning. His remains, interred at first in front of his beloved Church, rested there until the dismantling of the building in 1872, when Mrs. Jane Williamson, one of his daughters, caused their removal, and the same kind hands that first buried them (Mr. R. R. Shekell's) transferred them to the Presbyterian Cemetery and thence to Oak Hill, where Mr. W. W. Corcoran gave them a final resting place and a monumental tablet in the chapel.

Dr. Balch will yet be long remembered as a preacher of the old style, eccentric in his demeanor and at the same time remarkably genial in all his work and intercourse.

The congregation has been but for very limited times without a settled pastor. Dr. BALCH had as assistant, for a short time from the year 1823, Rev. JOHN CAMPBELL.⸬ In his declining health he had, as co-pastor, Rev. JOHN C. SMITH. At the Doctor's death, Sept. 7, 1833, Mr. Smith was called to the full pastorate, remaining with the Church until his acceptance of a call, April 9, 1839, to the FOURTH CHURCH, Washington. Rev. R. T. BERRY followed from October 3, 1841, to August 28, 1849 ; Rev. J. M. P. ATKINSON, from March 12, 1850, to February 12, 1856 ; Rev. Dr. J. H. BOCOCK, February 17, 1857, to May 27, 1861. Dr. B. F. BITTINGER then declining a call, Rev. F. T. BROWN was the pastor during the troublous times of the war—from second Sabbath, June, 1861, to February 6, 1865. June 21, 1865, Rev. A. A. E. TAYLOR was installed, and remained until May 3, 1869, succeeded by Rev. D. W. MOFFAT May 6, 1870, to April 10, 1872, and he, in May of that year, by Rev. S. H. Howe until 1883, when the pulpit, becoming again vacant, was supplied by Rev. T. S. Childs until the present pastor, Dr. Fullerton, entered on his charge in September of the same year.

During the times of the war for some months the church building, with others in Washington, was occupied by the Government as a hospital for the sick and wounded soldiery, and the congregation worshipped on alternate Sabbaths with the Methodist Protestant Church on Congress street. This was courteous reciprocity for a like Christian courtesy extended in years previous to the Methodist brethren when their building had been burned.

Under each of the pastorates from 1833 to 1872 the Bridge-street Church advanced in strength, notwithstanding the small advance in the population around it and the removal of many of its best members to other sections of the city. In the pastorates of Drs. Bocock, Atkinson, and Howe seasons of revival added a number of the young of the congregation to the membership. In 1871 the question of a removal became a necessary consideration, and the present site of the new Church was selected.

June 8, 1879, the new edifice was dedicated and Rev. Dr.

Howe installed pastor. The sermon was by Dr. D. W. Moffat, one of the former pastors.

The West-street congregation have found their present location productive of much gain to their attendance and growth. The removal was accompanied, as is usual in such cases, with many regrets and tender historic remembrances. The old walls had been witnesses to many conferences of the friends of Zion; many meetings of Synod, of Presbytery, and of Church sessions; many of the last Christian rites given to sainted ones on high. Patriotic memorial services commemorative of the two Presidents, Jefferson and Adams, who died on the same 4th of July, had also been attended in this building by a crowded audience. Historic associations, therefore, of every nature were clustered here. But the removal, as has been shown, was an act of necessity; and now, sanctioned as it has been by the blessing of the Master, it is fully acquiesced in by all.

The population of Georgetown has not as yet advanced in proportion to the increase in the eastern sections of the Capital. Additions to the membership of this church, therefore, continue to be looked for chiefly from the Sabbath Schools brought under the influence of the pulpit. These additions steadily continue and are still those of a character promising the most in healthful permanence. Full and attentive congregations attest the value of the Pastor's ministrations. The roll of church members reported to the Assembly of 1887 numbered 290, to which more than 30 additions have been recently made. Liberal contributions to the Boards appear in all the columns of the Minutes. The Sabbath Schools number 400. A mission school near the location of the Church of 1821, begun with promise last year under Mr. and Mrs. W. I. Lewis, has been transferred to the Church of the Covenant, the West street mission of Market street being still maintained. All of the Church properties, the building, Chapel, Manse and Mission are free from debt. Their value is estimated at $60,000. The Chapel with its lot and that of the Church, were the gifts of Messrs. Darby and Cissel when residents of Georgetown.

CHURCH OFFICERS:—Pastor, Rev. THOMAS FULLERTON, D. D., 3121 P St. (The Manse). Elders:—W. H. Dougal, A. Greenlees J. Leetch, B. R. Mayfield, F. L. Moore, C. S. Smith, J. A. Williamson. Deacons :—D. Auld, L. S. Frey, T. S. Gibbs, J. T. Swindells. Trustees :—C. Becker, W. D. Brace, S. T. Brown, W. M. Dougal, L. S. Frey, P. F. Gilbert, J. T. Motter, R. S. Tenney, W. W. Winship.

The venerable Journal of the Board of Trustees is a model for such records. It opens with a fair transcript of the Charter granted to the Church in 1806 by Congress, signed by Nathaniel Macon, Speaker of the House of Representatives, and S. Smith, President *pro tempore* of the Senate, and approved by Thomas Jefferson, President. Singularly enough, this charter, of which the parchment original is still preserved, restricts the revenues of the Church to the sum of $3,000. Among its later records is that of the deposits made in 1872, under the corner-stone of the new Church on West street with those then re-laid from the corner-stone of the old building of 1821.

The First Presbyterian Church, Four and One-half Street.—1795.

This church was the first of our organization within the limits of the " Federal City." Its earliest history indeed runs back to a date six years before the removal of the seat of Government from Philadelphia. The records of Baltimore Presbytery show that, at a stated meeting of that Presbytery, April 29, 1795, a call was presented " from the Churches in Washington for the services of Rev. JOHN BRECKINRIDGE;" and on the 24th of June following, at a called meeting at Bladensburg, on the report of " a committee respecting the Churches in said town and its vicinity," measures were taken for the future installation of this Minister.

It appears evident, then, that whatever is to be understood by the term " Churches " here used (probably as Rev. Mr. McFALLS considers " small bands of believers as yet without formal organization ") a Presbyterian society existed, and a regular pastoral relation was contemplated. As is well known, the so-called " Federal City " of that day was as yet one of a thinly scattered population. For ten years before the removal of the Government here, its area embraced scarcely 500 inhabitants. In 1801 Pennsylvania avenue was a deep morass covered with alder bushes. For years Senators and Representatives, by necessity, resided in Georgetown.

The first services for the new congregation were held in a carpenter's shop, put up for the use of the workmen employed in building the President's house, and when this was taken down, a frame chapel was erected on a lot on F street, near Saint Patrick's (Roman Catholic) Church, the use of the lot being temporarily given by Mr. David Burns, one of the original proprietors of land in the city. In 1803 the congregation was weakened by the gathering of the Church of the Associate Reformed Body under Rev. JAMES LAURIE. Mr. BRECKINRIDGE's services were, however, continued under his appointment from the General Assembly to this people and to those at Bladensburg; for a time the Washington services were held in the " Academy East."

Erection of the Church at the foot of Capitol Hill.

In the year 1810, Mr. George Blagden, Elias B. Caldwell, John Coyle, Daniel Rapine, and John McClelland, "formed themselves into a Committee to attempt the building of a house of worship." A subscription was opened and application for aid made to the General Assembly, with a statement of the desires of the people, that the Assembly would be pleased to continue the Mission while they would go forward with the building. The request was granted, and a new commission for Mr. Breckenridge issued through the Presbytery of Baltimore. Until the completion of this first house of worship, Divine Services were held, and the Sacraments administered, in the basement of the north wing of the Capitol; at the communion services the "metallic tokens" of that day were distributed. The Society was small and of moderate ability, but a subscription of $350 was made for the Minister.

June 25, 1812, the "Little White Church" under the Hill was entered, and its dedication sermon preached by Mr. Breckenridge, from Luke xix, 9: "This day is salvation come to this house." It was a plain brick structure on "South Capitol Street." Among the contributors to its erection were, President Madison, Hon. James Monroe, Wm. R. King, John Lambert, and Josiah Quincy. The first cost was but $4,000; the building was afterwards enlarged for an additional $3,000. In September, 1812, its Session held its first meeting.

Mr. Breckenridge was installed July 4, 1813, and continued to be the Pastor until the relation was dissolved in May, 1818. He died in 1844, at the age of 75, and was buried at the place then known as Harewood, where Mr. W. W. Corcoran, in after years, gave his remains a resting place. After his resignation of the Pastorate, the pulpit was supplied by Messrs. John McKnight, Andrew Hunter, and John Clark, until the call in April, 1819, to Rev. Reuben Post, who was ordained and installed June 24th of that year.

From the first forming of this Church the favor of God rested upon it, prompting in the hearts of the people an active missionary spirit.

The population of the Hill and its vicinity did not, however, grow as the original property-holders had expected. They held their property at such prices in what was then supposed would be the centralization of the future city as to force the bulk of the new residences much further westward. Other denominations also began to erect their houses of worship at no great distance from Mr. Post's charge. His pulpit and pastoral labors promised him large success if a new location should be secured " west of the Tiber Creek," as then called. The site of the present building on 4½ street, 108 feet front by 113 deep, was therefore purchased for 20 cents per foot, the building contract being for $8,000. The old edifice was sold to the African M. E. Society for $2,500. At the head of the subscribers for the new building was the name of Dr. Post for $500, his salary being but $1,000 per annum. The whole cost exceeded $12,000.

April 10, 1827, the corner-stone was laid, and the church dedicated December 9 of the same year, Dr. Post's sermon being from the appropriate text, Haggai ii, 9 : " The glory of the latter house shall be greater than that of the former." He was filled with the hope which is founded on the unfailing covenant of the Master to be with His people. Dr. Post was a minister of deep piety, who, although not distinguished for great pulpit ability, so faithfully followed up the ministrations of the Sabbath by personal visitations and converse that the Church received accessions, especially from the young men of the congregation, strengthening it for years after his resignation. The pastoral relation was dissolved by the Presbytery of the District, June 24, 1836, that Dr. Post might accept a call to the Independent Congregational Society of Charleston, in which city he died September 28, 1858.

After a brief supply of the pulpit by Rev. ADDISON MINES, and the declining of a call by Rev. WM. J. ARMSTRONG, Rev. W. McLAIN, of the New Haven Association, was installed Pastor January 11, 1837, and continued with the Church until failing health made his resignation necessary in 1840. He continned in the service of the Presbytery as its Stated Clerk, and also held the office of Secretary of the American Colonization Society until his death, February 13, 1873.

Mr. McLain's ministry was followed by that of Rev. Charles Rich, of the Hartford Association, who was installed November 30, 1840, but who also resigned by reason of ill health in the third year of his service. The pulpit was then supplied for a time by Rev. C. H. Nourse and others. In the fall of the same year Rev. William T. Sprole, of the Presbytery of Harrisburg, was installed, remaining with the Church until his appointment as Chaplain to the United States Military Academy in 1847, after which date, at their own request, the congregation were supplied by Presbyterian appointments until the installation of Rev. Elisha Ballentyne, of Prince Edward county, Virginia, March 1st, 1848, who also resigned on account of ill health in 1851. His people at his departure manifested their regret and their esteem for his services by the outward token of a purse of 2,000 dollars presented through Dr. William Gunton, President of the Board of Trustees. He died suddenly at Bloomington, Indiana, in 1886.

During these pastorates the Church was steadily strengthened; the attendance on the pulpit ministrations was always that of a large and interested audience; several revivals were granted, reminding the friends of the Church of the older seasons of such blessings. The Sabbath School, with its organized Juvenile Missionary Society, was sustained by an efficient corps of faithful teachers, and a mission work begun in a distant section of the city. Among the pew-holders were Presidents Polk and Pierce, Senators Benton, Buchanan, Wright and others, Hon. E. Whittelsey, Judge Collamer and General Cass.

The three elders named as laboring for the founding of the Church lived to see their hopes realized ; several of them through its prosperity of twenty-five years. Among those of long service are the names of Mr. James Moore, serving till 1853 ; Mr. Andrew Coyle, till 1855 ; Mrs. W. H. Campbell, 1840 till 1881 ; Mr. Leonidas Coyle, 1841 till 1866.

The present Pastor, Rev. Byron Sunderland, D. D., was unanimously elected, and installed April 21, 1853, his ministry now reaching through a period exceeding thirty-four years. Soon after his settlement an increased attendance made it necessary that the Church building be reconstructed by adding to its height, extending it to the rear of its grounds, elevating the audience room, and making a new front. Its sitting capacity, with its galleries, is now 1,000.

The re-dedication, December 9, 1860, was by the services of the venerable Dr. SPRING in the morning, Rev. C. H. READ in the afternoon, and Rev. J. JENKINS at night: these three Ministers representing thus the Old School, the New School, and the Southern Churches of that day.

The Church property is valued at $75,000. Friends outside and within the congregation presented the residence of the Pastor to him as a token of their esteem for his services. Invited in 1864–5 by the American and Foreign Christian Union to take charge of the American Chapel in Paris, Dr. SUNDERLAND was acting pastor of that Church on the Rue de Berri for about seventeen months, his people supplying their pulpit.

Since the year 1860, and until recently, several causes have operated to bring some embarrassment to this Church. The first was one which has a like history in all cities—the removal of a number of members from the immediate neighborhood; a further withdrawal occurring in 1866 by disaffection at the delivery by Mr. Frederick Douglass of a lecture in the Church.

By this the harmony of the congregation was impaired and the Church lost many of her members; fidelity to truth also compels the record, that many of those who had insisted on the delivery, and promised from it the best results, were among those who afterwards withdrew. The union of the Old School and the New, in 1870, still further added to the former losses by the change of membership on the part of those who now felt themselves equally at home in other organizations nearer to them.

Notwithstanding these embarrassments experienced equally by no other of our city Churches, the FIRST PRESBYTERIAN of to-day is strong and harmonious in its various activities, and is exerting a commanding influence on prominent men attending its worship. Its roll numbers 300, 43 having been received in 1886; its Sabbath Schools number 368; its contributions to our different Church agencies have exceeded $6,500.

The F Street Church, 1803.

Although the original organization here was not under one of our Presbyteries, it held to essentially the same doctrines and polity under the Associate Reformed Body. The earliest of its sessional records were burned with the Treasury building in 1829. Those beginning in 1819 state that in May, 1821, when a union was effected in Philadelphia between the General Assembly of the Presbyterian Church and the Associate Reformed Body in the United States, the Presbytery of the Associate Reformed was ordered to be thenceforth designated the Second Presbytery of Philadelphia; and, that at a meeting of the Synod of Philadelphia in 1823, the F Street Church was ordered to be enrolled in the Presbytery of the District of Columbia.

The Church had been formed in 1803. In March of that year, a number of Christians of the Associate Reformed Body, who had removed to Washington when it became the seat of Government, invited the Rev. James Laurie, of Edinburgh, then visiting them, on the recommendation of Dr. John Mason, of New York, to assist them in gathering a congregation; Dr. Laurie was installed Pastor in the year following. The city was, as yet, with scarcely an inhabitant or dwelling. Mr. Laurie was accustomed to relate that, when on his way thither, he had asked his driver how far off it was, he received the answer, "Sir, we have been driving *through it for two hours.*"

The friends of the organization could not report a rapid growth of the Church membership, but at the time of their union with the Presbytery of the District, the Session record that "amid many difficulties and discouragements the Church had been kept alive;" and they express the hope that it "would prosper long after they would be gathered to their fathers." The present state of their legacy demonstrates anew the unchanging fidelity of God to His covenanting people.

The support of Mr. Laurie from his congregation being insufficient, he held for a long time a position in the Register's office, Treasury Department. He travelled North and South, collecting funds for the erection of the Church, having at the first occupied for divine service a room in the Treasury building. In 1815 he received the degree of Doctor of Divinity from Williams College, Massachusetts.

His pastorate, like those of his friends, Dr. Balch, and Dr. Harrison of the First Church, Alexandria, extended over a long period; his for fifty-three years. April 10th, 1853, at a Communion season, he alluded very feelingly to his approaching decease, saying, " The time cannot be far off," and adding, as he leaned over his pulpit, almost in a whisper, " I feel it." On the Sabbath following he sent word to his choir the request to sing the hymn, " Jerusalem, my happy home," and in a few hours closed a life of 75 years with the words, " It is well." He was a preacher of the old regime, doctrinal, yet clear and affectionate, his pastoral work also being remarkably tender and faithful to all. The Session of 1853 record their deep sense of the loss of one of the best pastors and best of citizens.

The original elders were Joseph Nourse, John McGowan, and Alexander McDonald. A number of the officers of the Government were the early friends and members of this Church.

During the later years of Dr. Laurie's ministry the following co-Pastors were successively elected to that office: Rev. Septimus Tustin, 1839 to 1845; Rev. Ninian Bannatyne, from 1845 to 1848, the year of his lamented death; Rev. L. H. Christian, 1850; and Rev. D. X. Junkin, in the same year, remaining until his resignation and appointment as Chaplain in U. S. Navy in 1853. March 2, 1854, Rev. Phineas D. Gurley was installed Pastor by the Presbytery of Baltimore, under his ministry the union between the F Street and the Second Presbyterian Church was happily effected. The history of this Church therefore finds its next place here.

The Second Presbyterian Church of 1820.

The sessional records of this organization, dated May 9, 1820, state that, under the advisement of the Presbytery of Baltimore, forty-one persons, whose names appear on the record, then formed themselves into a congregation. On the 13th of October following Rev. J. T. Russel constituted the Church, its first Elders being Messrs. John Craven and Joseph Brumley. June 6, 1821, Rev. Daniel Baker, of the Presbytery of Winchester, was elected

Pastor. His work, which was one of largely-extended usefulness, was closed by his resignation to accept a call, 1828, to the Independent Presbyterian Church of Savannah, when the pulpit was declared vacant by Rev. Dr. Post, March 30, 1828.

After Rev. Luther Halsey, of Princeton, had declined a subsequent call by the Church, Dr. J. N. Campbell, of Albany, served them as Stated Supply until the fall of 1830, from which last-named date to the year 1845 they were under the short pastorates successively of Revs. E. H. Smith, P. H. Fowler, George Wood, R. W. Clark, W. W. Eels, and J. Knox, after whom the pulpit was filled by temporary supplies only until the call in 1849 to Rev. James R. Eckard. His useful pastorate closed in 1853. A short supply by Rev. J. D. Matthews followed, the Church having transferred its relation under Dr. Eckard from the Presbytery of the District to the Presbytery of Baltimore.

From the date of this transfer the pulpit was supplied by Rev. Dr. James G. Hamner until the union with the F Street Church.

The Union of July 30, 1859,

was a most necessary and useful result, not only as effecting the basis of a more successful and permanent church work than could be expected from the past experience or the existing state of either of the two churches, but as terminating, in the case of the Second Church, a long series of struggles to secure entire unity of action among devout and zealous workers. From the good old days of Daniel Baker's lamented resignation of the pastorate this lack of unity was apparent. It grew chiefly out of too rigid an adherence to things in church polity not essential to true prosperity. The details of this need not be quoted here from the church records. The building originally occupied was one of the most unpretending character; yet, under the blessing of God, it had been the birth-place of many souls. Dr. Baker's ministry, especially, was one of marked success. His devoted spirit manifested itself through the whole of his pastorate—a spirit which afterwards made his name so revered in the Southwest as the winner of souls for his Master. Among his first trustees were President Adams and Secretary Southard. Mr. Adams was a regular attendant, for a long time taking a lively interest in the church. He loaned to it, when under difficulty, a sum of money conditionally on receiving no interest. President Jackson was, for a time, a pew-holder.

At the date of the union with the present N. Y. Avenue Church the Elders were Michael Nourse, Charles Stott, John M. McCalla, and William Waller. At a communion service October 14, 1859, seventy-four members united, by certificate, with the F Street Church. The Presbytery of Potomac then struck from its rolls the separate names of the two former organizations. This action resulted in the selling of the building upon F street and the erection of a fine edifice on New York avenue, on a lot which the Second Church had previously owned. A strong church of wealth, enterprise, and zeal was developed, through which Presbyterianism enlarged its borders in the National Capital. From it a colony went out, in 1865, and established the North Presbyterian Church. Next came the establishment of the Gurley Mission, and, later, another mission in the southern part of the city.

New York Avenue Church.

Dr. Gurley, who had been largely instrumental in securing the Union, now merged his pastorate of the F Street Church into that of the united congregations. His ministry, in Washington, of 14 years, was closed by death September 30, 1868. A man of God, of deep piety and usefulness, his labors had justly placed him at the head of some of the most important committees of the whole church of which he was the guiding officer as Moderator of the Assembly of 1867. He had been the confidential friend of more than one of our Presidents; he was the friend and pastor of President Lincoln, enjoyed the love and confidence of that great and good man, whose death-bed he attended, the family and Cabinet of whom he comforted, whose funeral services, in the East Room of the Executive Mansion, he conducted, and whose remains he accompanied to their quiet resting-place in Illinois. He was, also, chaplain, for a number of years, of the House of Representatives. Among his last words at the close of a lingering and most painful disease, was a new message of love to his people, and an expression of like spirit to the brethren around his bed: "I love you all."

In November, 1869, Rev. S. S. Mitchell, of Harrisburg, was

installed pastor, and at his release in 1878, to accept a call to the Reformed Church in Brooklyn, Rev. J. R. Paxton was installed, and remained with the Church until February 19, 1882.

The present Pastor, Dr. William Alvin Bartlett was installed October 24th of the same year.

The prosperity of this church which holds so important a position at the capital continues to be of a very marked character. The Sessional report for the year ending March 10, 1887, records a larger attendance during the year and a greater number of its members engaged in some branch of its activities than at any previous date of its history. The membership had been increased by 73 names; 68 on profession : the total number 831. Vacancies caused by dismissions during the past two years of the large number who chiefly formed the new "Church of the Covenant" had been almost immediately more than filled. Totals of contributions to the nine Boards of the Assembly footed up nearly $2,000; those for other benevolent agencies $5,200; and the aggregate of receipts by the Trustees, Session, and the different societies of the church work, $27,115. Improvements placed upon the building and on the Manse had cost $12,000. The estimated value of all the properties held by the Trustee is in excess of $100,000.

The spiritual prosperity of the Church is received as the answer to the prayers of Pastor and people on the ministrations of the pulpit and on pastoral visitations. The number of societies working in the Church itself and in the missions of Bethany Chapel and Gurley Mission attests also the good spirit which, under God's blessing, prevails.

CHURCH OFFICERS.—*Pastor*, William Alvin Bartlett, D. D., 1201 K street, The Manse; *Elders*, C. B. Bailey, H. A. Claughton, S. L. Crissey, J. W. Foster, S. F. Phillips, N. A. Robbins, J. Randolph, C. B. Walker, H. H. Wells; *Deacons*, F. O. Beckett, C. H. Merwin, L. S. Emery, C. E. Foster, J. R. Imbrie, P. F. Larner, C. S. Bradley, R. P. A. Denham, B. Taylor, W. B. Gurley, J. D. McChesney, J. R. VanMeter; *Superintendent of Church Sabbath-School*, J. R. VanMeter; *Superintendent of Gurley Mission Sabbath-School*, N. A. Robbins; *Trustees*, J. P. Chapman, L. Clephane, W. Thompson, N. D. Larner, J. W. Thompson, J. W. Douglas, W. M. Galt, B. H. Warner.

The Fourth Church, 9th Street, 1828.

The organization of this Church was the result of some dissatisfaction entertained, by members of the old " Second Church," with the means alleged to have been employed in the election of a successor to the Rev. Daniel Baker, at the time of his resignation of the pastorate, 1828. The objections, it is believed, were chiefly against the use of *proxies.* October 29th of that year, twenty-three of these members, meeting at the house of Mr. Jacob Gideon, associated themselves in a new organization to be known as " the Central Presbyterian Society," the Rev. Joshua N. Danforth to be their Pastor and Mr. David M. Wilson their Ruling Elder. In January 1829, they were enrolled under the care of the Presbytery of the District as " the Fourth Presbyterian Church," and leave granted them to employ the services of Rev. Mr. Danforth, who was received in April of the year following from the Presbytery of Newcastle. Their first church building was a very unpretending one, on the east side of the street on which the present house stands. It was dedicated March 1st of the preceding year, Rev. John Breckenridge, of Kentucky, officiating.

The ministry of Mr. Danforth was much blessed, extending to the year 1832, when Rev. Mason Noble was installed, under whose ministry the church was further enlarged in numbers, and its influence extended in the city. On the release of Mr. Noble, Sept., 11 1839, to accept a call to the Eleventh Church in New York, the pulpit was supplied by Rev. J. L. Bartlett until, in September of the same year, having made a unanimous call to Rev. John C. Smith, of the Bridge-street, Georgetown, he was installed by the Presbytery of the District. Dr. Smith's ministry extended through the long period of nearly forty years. It was one of fruitful increase to the membership and influence of the Church. His previous experiences in the service of the " Domestic Missionary Society of Richmond, and his pastoral work in Portsmouth, Virginia, and in Georgetown had been characterized by the same spirit of devout consecration that now showed itself through the whole period of his labors for the Fourth Church. Declining a call to a pastorate in Philadelphia, Dr. Smith entered on a most active work to promote the spiritual state of his new charge. A series of meetings, protracted through months of solicitude, resulted in the addition of nearly fifty new members.

The increase of the congregation early demanded the erection of a larger house of worship, the corner-stone of which was laid June 24, 1840, and the Church dedicated free from debt on the 20th of June, of the year following. On that occasion, Rev. Edward Kirk, of Boston, Rev. John Mines and Rev. William McLain assisted the Pastor. Early in Dr. Smith's Ministry he arranged a plan of Pastoral Visitation by which he faithfully visited every family in the Church three times in the year; referring to which, in a sermon to his people in 1845, he said: " My " books will show that I have carefully executed my plan; I can " tell where I have been and what I have been doing for the last " twenty-five years; I am going to the judgment seat of Christ " with these records. I renew to-day my consecration." When the late war began and the national troops were arriving in the city, he immediately took his stand for the Union.

He made the duties of the hour the subject of a special appeal to his people, and soon entered on the additional labors of visiting the sick and wounded in the different hospitals of the city.

Disabled partially from the active duties of the pulpit during the years immediately preceding his death, he enlisted the services of Rev. Joseph T. Kelly, as co-Pastor, who entered on these duties May 5, 1874, and succeeded to the full pastorate at the death of Dr. Smith, Jan'y 23, 1878.

CHURCH RECORD.

Organized 24th November, 1828. *Pastors and Stated Supplies:* Rev. J. N. Danforth, S. S., from organization to April, 1832; Rev. Mason Noble, Pastor, from June, 1832, to 11th September, 1839; Rev. John C. Smith, Pastor, 27th September, 1839, to 23d January, 1878; Rev. J. T. Kelly, Pastor, 5th May, 1874. *Elders—Class of* 1889—Robert S. Jordan, Daniel McFarlan, Thomas McGill;—*Class of* 1888—Joseph A. Sterling, John B. Sleman;—*Class of* 1887—Henry J. Hunt. Joseph A. Sterling, Clerk; Robert S. Jordan, Treasurer. *Trustees*—D. P. Wolhaupter, Frank L. Middleton, John A. Prescott, Robert H. Harkness, John W. Hollyday.

The Fifteenth Street Church.--1841.

This Church was founded in the labors and prayers of Elder D. M. Wilson, formerly of the Second Presbyterian organization, and those of Rev. John F. Cook. Mr. Cook was hopefully converted in the prayer meetings held through Mr. Wilson's instrumentality, and following the example and efforts of Mr. Wilson, who was among the first to labor for the religious good of the colored people of Washington, began in 1842 to gather his friends in a Sabbath School on H and Fourteenth Street, enlisting them in the hope, also, of organization as a Church. This was effected May 14, 1842, by an enrollment on the lists of the Presbytery of the District of Columbia, as "the First Colored Presbyterian Church of Washington."

Forty communicants of this organization worshipped in "Cook's school-house," at the location just named, until they were enabled by the assistance of the First, Second and Fourth Churches to build a small frame on the site of their present Church. Rev. J. C. Smith was from the first their warm friend and helper by his counsels and contributions. He preached the sermon at the ordination and installation of Mr. Cook, July 14, 1843.

The narratives of the Church, embodied in the report of the Presbytery to the General Assembly in 1849 and 1853, speak most encouragingly of the growth and prospects of the people, the erection of their present edifice on Fifteenth Street having been then begun.

The congregation under Mr. Cook's labors had very largely increased, but the faithful pastor was worn down by the efforts made for his Church while at the same time engaged in the laborious daily duties of a teacher. He was called to his reward in the year 1855.

From this date, Revs. W. Catto, in 1858, and B. F. Tanner, in 1861, were installed Pastors, and the Church, in 1864, becoming vacant, was supplied for several months chiefly by Rev. W. B. Evans, until the installation of Mr. H. H. Garnett, whose pastoral relation was dissolved October 3, 1866. After the stated supply by Rev. J. H. Muse, Rev. Sella Martin was Pastor from December 27, 1868, to February 18, 1870, when the Church again becoming vacant was regularly supplied by Dr. S. Tustin until the settlement of Rev. G. VanDeurs in 1874, followed by that of Rev. J. Brown, 1875, and F. J. Grimke, 1878 to 1885.

After Mr. Grimke's resignation in 1885, the pulpit was filled by Rev. C. H. A. Buckley, D. D., one of the Professors of Howard University, by appointment of Presbytery Moderator, - also of the Session. January 18, 1887, Rev. J. R. Riley, of Louisville, Kentucky, was installed, Rev. Dr. Bartlett preaching the sermon; the charges to Pastor and people being delivered by Rev. Dr. Sunderland and Rev. J. E. Nourse.

The Report of this charge to the General Assembly of 1887 gives a roll of 210 members; of the Sabbath School an equal number. Total of moneys raised during the year for congregational and benevolent agencies, $1,638. The Church holds an important position as the only one among our colored people in Washington under the influence of the educated Ministry of our Church. Its Pastors have been men of sound theological training. Its influence may be expected to be that of solid principles and warm piety among a large membership and attendance.

The pastorate was again vacated December 28, '87.

Elders, David Fisher, H. F. Grant, James Meriwether, Henry W. Lee.

Trustees, F. J. Shadd, F. L. Cardoza, W. D. Montague, Joseph Morrison, Aaron Russell, J. T. Gaskins, J. R. Francis, W. T. Crusor, W. A. Stuart.

The building on 15th street was erected and furnished largely by the aid of our other Churches here. It holds a central and commanding position, and is worth over $55,000.

The Assembly Church, March 9, 1853, 5th and I Streets.

The present name of this Church was authorized by the Presbytery of the District of Columbia, in 1855, in commemoration of the previous meeting of the General Assembly (N. S.), in Washington. It had been enrolled in 1853 as the Fifth Church.

For months previous to its organization, prayer meetings had been continuously held by Elder D..M. Wilson of the Fourth Church, sustained by the hearty support of his Pastor, Rev. J. C. Smith, and by the labors of Messrs. Stansbury, Bogan, and Clements, members of that Church. The organization embraced but 20 members over whom Rev. Andrew G. Carothers was installed Pastor, and Messrs. John Douglas and John T. Clements Ruling Elders.

Contributions for the new church were received from 22 States of the Union.

In November, 1860, Mr. Carother s'health failing him, he was released to seek restoration in a Southern climate, but died in 1863, on the Island of Martinique, W. I.

In May of the year following, Rev. Thaddeus B. McFalls, who had been received by the Presbytery from the Methodist Episcopal body, was installed as Mr. Carothers' successor, but his health also failing he was released December 10, 1867. His strength had been much impaired by his services as Chaplain during the war; he died in Washington, at the early age of 38, May 22, 1873, having fulfilled most faithfully the services also of Stated Clerk of the Presbytery from its organization of the consolidated body in 1870.

After the brief pastorate of Rev. Wm. Hart, 1868 to 1870, a union was effected October 5th of that year, under Dr. Charles Boynton, then Pastor of "the Central Congregational Church" on 8th street, between the members of that Church (then disbanded) and those of the Assembly's.

Dr. Boynton was installed over the united congregation, and remained with it until his release to accept a call to Cincinnati in 1873.

The present pastor, Rev. George O. Little, was called by the Church June 1 of the last-named year.

The Annual Report presented in the Church Manual for 1887 states that, under God's blessing, long experienced harmony and activity in Church work continues; the financial condition of the Church being also in advance of that of previous years. The membership reported to the Assembly is 337. Contributions to the various Church agencies exceed $1,000; the columns for our Boards in the minutes of the Assembly being all well filled. The Sabbath-School roll shows a membership of 357; 57 of the scholars being church members. The attendance of the scholars on the pulpit administrations was an average of 58 per cent. of the whole number. The Library of the School, under the care of Mr. James C. Strout, is probably the model for its keeping, and its records show the number of volumes to be 2,361.

OFFICERS.—Rev. Geo. O. Little, Pastor. *Elders:* W. J. Redstrake, L. Holtzlander, Chas. Lyman, N. B. Bartlett, Thos. P. Keene, O. B. Brown. *Deacons:* F. L. Campbell, L. C. Williamson. *Trustees:* Thomas R. Senior, W. M. Boyd, A. M. McBath, L. C. Williamson, Chas. M. Robinson, Christian Dickey; Geo. H. Read, Treasurer.

The Church organization was the fruit of the abundant labors of Rev. Mason Noble, who held in 1851 a series of prayer-meetings in private residences in South Washington, chiefly in those of Messrs. Knight, Hercus, and Thompson.

These meetings gave such promise as to call for public Sabbath services, which were held first August 28, 1852, in " Island Hall;" a Sabbath-School of 50 members being also opened. January 23, 1853, at a meeting presided over by Dr. Noble, 32 members were enrolled, electing Mr. John Knight Ruling Elder; and on the second Sabbath of February, at the first Communion service, these were joined in fellowship by members of First, Second, and Fourth Churches.

Dr. Noble, though unable to accept installation, by reason of his position as Chaplain in the United States Navy, served the Church in the full ministrations of his office from the date named until 1855, and resumed his labors on his return from sea duty, 1858 to 1862; and again from 1870 to his lamented death, October 24, 1881.

During his first absence the pulpit depended on the Supply by Rev. B. F. Morris. Rev. Geo. H. Smyth was Pastor, 1864 to 1869; and Rev. Geo. P. Noble, Stated Supply from 1869 until Dr. Noble's second return from sea duty. Dr. Noble's labors were abundantly blessed, and the Church under his successors, though composed of members in moderate circumstances only, has kept its good standing in the community. His name is much revered.

Rev. Frank H. Burdick, September 27, 1882, was elected Pastor, and installed 23d April, 1884, resigning in 1887.

The present Pastor, Rev. Scott F. Hershey, Ph. D., was installed October 5, 1887.

The roll of Communicants numbers 165; Sabbath-School, 150; value of Church, property and manse, $40,000.

OFFICERS.—Rev. Scott F. Hershey, Ph. D., Pastor. *Elders :* Ros. A. Fish, Jacob De Pue, Geo. C. Hercus. *Trustees :* Charles B. Pearson, Ros. A. Fish, Wm. A. Thompson, Jno. G. Thompson, Clark B. Philips, Jas. C. Lee, Howard S. Reeside.

In his historical discourse, delivered October 3, 1886, by the Pastor of this Church, Rev. Dr. Benjamin F. Bittinger, he speaks thus of its founding:

" In the year 1851, certain friends interested in Church extension, and principally connected with the F Street Church, had their attention directed to the growing population of this section of the city, as an inviting field for the establishment of a Church holding our doctrines and conforming to our form of worship and government. Among these were Rev. James Laurie, D. D., and Rev. David X. Junkin, D. D., Pastors of the F Street Church ; Rev. John M. P. Atkinson, D. D., Pastor of the Bridge Street Church, Georgetown, D. C.; and Messrs. Charles Stott, F. A. Tschiffely, Edward M. Clarke, and Gilbert Cameron, members of the F Street Church.

" After examination of the field and consultation among these gentlemen, it was decided to bring the matter to the notice of the Presbytery of Baltimore, who gave their sanction and promised co-operation and aid in conducting the enterprise.

" At first, religious services were held in the Columbia Engine House, near the Capitol, in the morning of the Sabbath, and in Potomac Hall, corner of Eleventh street and Maryland avenue, at night. The congregations gradually grew in numbers, a Sabbath-School was gathered, and on the 14th of June, 1853, a Church was organized, under the name and title of the Seventh Street Church, of Washington City. The name was suggested by the fact that the site chosen for the erection of a Church edifice was on that street ; the site being generously donated by Mr. Charles Stott. In December, 1873, by a vote of the congregation, approved by the Presbytery, this name was changed to Westminster, by which, as an incorporated body, it is now known and called."

Mr. Isaac H. Wailes and Mr. John K. Woods were elected the first Elders ; Mr. E. Lycett and Mr. E. M. Clark, deacons. Two years afterwards, Mr. Wailes having died, Dr. J. D. Stewart and Messrs. Daniel Davidson and Alexander Garden were elected.

Pastors and Stated Supplies.

Rev. John M. Henry, installed in 1853, was released by reason of ill health, in 1855, having by his consecrated zeal and devotion endeared himself to his people. His pastorate was succeeded by the brief service of Rev. E. B. Cleghorn, following whom, Rev. Dr. B. F. Bittinger, then Pastor of the Church at Lewinsville, Virginia, accepted a call and was installed March 12, 1857. The pulpit becoming again vacant by his removal to Ellicott's Mills, in June, 1863, Rev. William Y. Brown and Rev. W. W. Campbell were successively its Stated Supplies, the latter of whom was installed Pastor in 1865; on his release, 1867, Dr. Bittinger was again invited, and was installed January 5, 1868.

Though not maintained by a wealthy congregation the work of the Church has received a very marked influence through the liberality of its membership and friends, as shown by their outlays, at different periods, on improvements of the building and the purchase of the Manse, 638 F Street S.W.

The collections of the Mite Society alone have reached the sum of $11,000. The Church properties, valued at $15,000, are entirely free from debt. Regularity of attendance on the ministrations of the pulpit and the interest shown in the different branches of the work of the Church commend themselves to the people. The whole pastoral relation manifestly has been, and is, productive of permanent growth. In Dr. McFall's MSS., he writes: "Dr. Bittinger has been very successful in his present " charge. He has an intelligent and devoted people who are " ready to assist him in his plans of usefulness." From its first organization the Church has received to its membership 415 persons; 212 by profession. Number reported to the Assembly of 1887, 151; of Sabbath School scholars, 165. The columns given in the minutes, for contributions to the Boards, are all filled.

OFFICERS OF THE CHURCH.—*Pastor*, Benjamin F. Bittinger, D. D., 638 F street S.W. (The Manse); *Ruling Elders*, Alexander Garden, Daniel D. Davidson, Charles B. Church, Abraham Depue; *Deacons*, Samuel W. K. Handy, Thomas Taylor; *Trustees:* Joseph M. Wilson, President; J. Whitley Herron, Secretary; Abraham Depue, Treasurer; David E. Holmes, Albert G. Yount, Lawrence H. Hopkins, William A. H. Church, Oliver O. Spicer, George Messer.

The Western Presbyterian Church.—1855.

This Church, like the Assembly's and the Fifteenth Street, owes its foundation under God to the devoted labors of Elder David M. Wilson, of the Fourth Church. As early as 1848, with the experience gained by this servant of the Master in the Sabbath-School, the Tract and the Bible cause, he commenced missionary labors in the " First Ward," holding prayer-meetings first in private houses near the Old Glass House, and next at a Chapel erected near the corner of 22d and E streets. A Sabbath-School was opened and two weekly services held. The work meeting with the Divine favor, as shown by a number of hopeful conversions, application was early made to the Presbytery for the organization of a Church, and in April, 1854, an invitation was extended to Rev. T. N. Haskell, of the Union Theological Seminary, to become the Pastor. He preached his first sermon May 14 of the same year.

In August the corner-stone of a house of worship was laid, Rev. Drs. Smith and Sunderland officiating, and pledging with others their hearty support. January 13 a formal organization was made, twenty-four members being enrolled, about one-half by certificate from the Fourth Church, the rest on profession. Rev. Mr. Haskell was elected Pastor and Mr. Wilson Ruling Elder. Mr. Haskell was ordained and installed in the month of February.

The first trustees were Messrs. W. F. Steiger, A. W. Denham, T. F. Harkness, and C. H. VanPatten. The new enterprise sustained a most serious loss in the death (February 26, 1856) of Elder Wilson, to whose memory is due the record of one of his Pastors in the words, " He was the most heavenly-minded man I ever knew."

The Church edifice was completed and dedicated June 17, 1857. In the year succeeding, a season of gracious refreshing was enjoyed, adding a number to the Communion of the Church. Rev. T. N. Haskell resigned his pastorate May 11, 1858, and from this date to April of the following year the pulpit was supplied principally by Prof. Huntington, of Columbian College.

Rev. J. R. Bartlett, installed August 31, 1859, removed to the

South at the beginning of the late war; in March, 1862, Rev. J. N. Coombs, who had been a Minister in the Methodist Church, was received from that body and installed. The violent death of Mr. Coombs, by his own hands, during a time of mental aberration, December 27, 1874, was a most lamented and serious blow to the Church. During his pastorate, as many as 40 names had been added to its membership, and his Ministry and Presbyterian services had been those of acknowledged devotion to the work of the Master; the building had been remodeled and refurnished. Mr. Coombs' funeral services were largely attended. By his amiable manners and devoted zeal he had greatly endeared himself to the people and the community.

March 1, 1875, Rev. Dr. David Wills, of the Presbytery of Marion, Georgia, was elected Pastor and installed, May 9th of that year remaining until January 28, 1878. During his Ministry, Dr Wills gave to his people a carefully prepared, and very interesting, history of the work of the Church from the time of its organization. "Since that time 373 had been in its connection; 188, received on profession. All of the first members except four had 'fallen on sleep.'" Dr. Wills entered on the duties of Chaplain in the United States Army; he is now the Pastor of a Church in Philadelphia.

The present Pastor, Rev. T. S. Wynkoop, was installed Octo. 23, 1878. His work continues to be that of a Minister eminently successful in pulpit Ministrations and Visitation among the people. The Minutes of the Assembly show a large increase in the power of the Church, which holds an important position as the only one of our faith and order in this part of the city.

The roll of Communicants numbers 290, and the different organizations for Church work prove its spiritual activity.

Additions during the year 1886, 21; the columns given to the Boards of Church in the Minutes are each largely filled.

OFFICERS.—*Pastor*, Rev. T. S. Wynkoop; *Elders*, C. D. Drake, J. W. Easby, W. H. H. Smith, J. T. Sweetman; *Deacons*, L. C. Denham, J. C. Allen, R. Armour, H. P. Catell, J. A. Wortham, W. H. Fearson; *Trustees*, G. H. McIlhany, M. R. Throop, R. Armour, A. Webster, J. C. Allen, J. B. Lambie, C. F. Moore, W. C. Bickford, J. J. Gregg.

Metropolitan Presbyterian Church, Fourth and B Streets Southeast.

Originally called the Capitol Hill Presbyterian Church, this organization resulted from the earnest desire of a few active Christians in that section of the city for a church based upon the doctrines and form of government of our Westminster standards. The growth of this section had already begun, yet, since the removal of the First Presbyterian Church in 1827 to Four-aud-a-half street N.W., no efforts had been made for the establishment of a Presbyterian Church on the Hill until the visits of Rev. Dr. John Chester in 1864.

Dr. Chester's first services were held February 28, 1864, in a school-building near Dudington Place, the attendants being 25 in number.

Although started in the war times, the indications of Providence were so encouraging that, on the 11th of April, the Presbytery of Potomac organized a church of 34 members, and installed Dr. Chester as Pastor, Rev. Dr. Gurley preaching the sermon, Drs. Tustin and Brown delivering the charges to the people and Pastor. Mr. Chas. E. Lathrop and Mr. Robt. Leitch were elected Elders, and Messrs. J. R. Arrison, J. T. Burchard, and James Simpson, Deacons.

The organization was in a larger school-room, 3d and A streets southeast. During the summer, by invitation of Hon. B. B. French, Commissioner of Public Buildings, the congregation worshipped in the Capitol in the Rooms of the Post Office Committee of the House of Representatives. Large audiences attended, and the Ordinances of Baptism and the Lord's Supper were here administered.

February 12, 1865, the first frame Chapel, 30 x 50 feet, was dedicated on the site of the present edifice, entirely free from debt. Its materials had been prepared in Burlington, N. J., Dr. Chester's former pastorate residence. Its cost with that of the lot was $4,000. Members of the congregation and of other Presbyterian churches in Washington contributed this money. A Sabbath School was begun in it February, 1865, with 210 scholars. This number, as well as that of the congregation, rapidly increasing, it soon became evident that a larger building would be required ; in February, 1869, the corner-stone of the present edifice was laid.

The very marked success, which the favor of God had thus shown to this work, now prompted the Presbytery of Potomac to overture the General Assembly to incorporate with the Church the proceeds of the property on E Street, N.W., which had been long held in the expectancy of establishing there a Metropolitan Church. The transfer of this, valued at $27,000, was ordered by the General Assembly of 1868. Long delays, however, occurred in the course of this transfer and in the building of the present edifice. The name of the Church was then changed to that of the Metropolitan Presbyterian.

December 8, 1872, the Dedication took place, and by the Spring of 1878 the Pastor had the pleasure of announcing in a historical discourse that the property was entirely free from debt. At that date the organization of 1864 with 34 members, had added 521 members, 255 on profession.

It has been made evident to the visitors to this Church during the ten years which have passed since the delivery of this Pastor's "Jubilee" sermon that no other people within the bounds of the Presbytery have been more favored with seasons of refreshing from on High. The additions which have been continuously made to the membership have been the results of the regular ministry of the pulpit and of pastoral visitations, which promise more of solidity and permanence than from occasional extra measures for reviving the work of God among His people and among the unconverted. They have been numerous. The population of the vicinity and its borders has also steadily increased, opening up the opportunity for the establishment of a Mission further East, out of which a new enterprise is looked for.

By the generous donation, chiefly of the late General William McK. Dunn, and under the care of the Presbyterian Alliance of this city, a lot has been purchased for the future erection of a Church ; a Mission Sabbath-School, which originated under the combined effort of the Metropolitan and Eastern Presbyterian Churches, is now wholly maintained and conducted by the Metropolitan Church. It is sufficient testimony to the results of the enterprise begun in 1864, that, at this day, under the bless ing of God, a colony can be spared for this new effort without harming the Metropolitan Church.

The minutes of the General Assembly for 1887 show a roll of members, 505, and of Sabbath scholars, 637. Columns of contributions to the agencies of the Assembly are all well filled, the total of moneys for all objects exceeding the sum of 8,500 dollars.

OFFICERS.—Rev. John Chester, D. D., Pastor. *Elders :* R. Leitch, J. R. Zimmerman, W. H. Barstow, J. Ridout, M. Van Ness, John C. Baxter, Edie Pollock, Theodore Swazey. *Deacons :* W. H. Clum, H. K. Simpson, J. H. O'Donnell, J. H. Beatty, W. Dubois, F. Aldrich, G. P. Bohrer, W: T. Van Doren. *Trustees :* J. Ridout, J. Burrows, G. N. West, C. T. Stewart, W. R. Russell, F. A. Grant, E. C. Fawcett, T. G. Jones, D. F. McGowan.

A number of members of the New York Avenue Church, chiefly those residing in the section of the city formerly called the Northern Liberties, having previously to the year 1865 interested themselves in the work of a Sabbath-School, there presented to the Presbytery of Potomac the question of organizing a Presbyterian Church. In reply, the Presbytery appointed Rev. Wm. Y. Brown and Gen'l E. C. Carrington a Committee on this subject, recommended that all the Presbyterian families of the neighborhood should identify themselves with the enterprise, and assured them of moral and material aid.

March 15, of the same year, at a meeting held in the school-house, 10th and M streets, a full conference of the representatives of these families resulted in a request for aid from the Session of the N. Y. Avenue Church to establish a Mission and erect a building for a Sabbath-School and for prayer-meetings. The chief promoters of the enterprise were Rev. Dr. Gurley and Messrs. Kerr, Ballantyne, Shepherd, Tschiffeley, Winslow, Ramsdell, Roberts, Musser, and Smith. They found a ready hearing from the Session, which authorized the purchase of a lot, and the employment of a Missionary. Under the care of Rev. L. R. Fox, a Church of 23 members was organized Dec. 4th, and Mr. Fox installed Pastor Dec. 31, 1865. A Church edifice, costing with its lots (N, between 9th and 10th streets N. W.) $8,750, had been dedicated Dec. 3d.

Under the ministry of six years of Rev. Mr. Fox, 128 members were added to the Communion, 36 on profession. The pastoral relation was dissolved Dec. 26, 1871. Under the succeeding Pastorates of Rev. J. G. Mason, Oct. 24, 1872, to Dec. 28, 1874, 47 members were received; 21 on profession.

The present Pastor, Rev. Chas. B. Ramsdell, was installed by the Presbytery of Washington City, Dec. 13, 1875; since which date 253 members have been received; 122 by profession. The whole number of the membership has thus resulted in an aggregate of 457; of whom 182, on profession. In 1878 the original building was much enlarged at the cost of $5,000. The total value of the property is estimated at $26,500, and is wholly free from debt.

At present, the Church is sustained by voluntary contributions, finding this system preferable to the former methods of pew rents. Systematic benevolence has been lately reintroduced with good results. The seating capacity of the Church is about 500; its lot large enough to admit the erection of a suitable front for a much needed lecture and Sunday-School room. The roll of communicants numbers 150; of Sabbath-School members, 202.

OFFICERS OF THE CHURCH.—*Pastor*, Rev. Charles B. Ramsdell. *Elders*, Samuel Ker, J. P. Jones, John L. Brown, C. H. Carrington, J. B. Linton. *Deacons*, George McKimmie, George J. Davis, Samuel J. Armstrong. *Trustees*, C. B. Ramsdell, R. Duryee, John G. Townsend, E. H. Chamberlin, Walter M. Pumphrey, Charles T. Caldwell, R. W. Hobson.

The Church owes its founding to the blessing of God upon an awakening in 1871, in Dr. Smith's Church, Ninth Street, of a renewed interest in the cause of Home Missions, which took the direction of inquiries as to a work of evangelization within the city limits. At the urgent request of Mr. F. C. Cate, a member of that Church, a committee appointed for such inquiry selected a location north of East Capitol Street, near where the present building stands.

June 11th, of the year named, a Sabbath School was opened with an attendance of thirteen scholars, in a private residence, Mr. F. C. Cate being elected Superintendent, with Mr. R. H. T. Liepold as his Assistant, and Mr. B. H. Warner, Librarian and Treasurer. Mr. Moses Kelly, one of the Elders of the Fourth Church, donated five lots on Eighth Street, on which, with aid from other first friends of the enterprise in 1872, a frame Chapel was erected. June 18th, of that year, religious services were begun, the attendance on the Sabbath School having rapidly increased and the private residence being too straitened for either this or for divine services.

Rev. J. T. Kelly, then completing his studies at the Theological Seminary of Princeton, was engaged to supply the pulpit and continued with the congregation until his election as co-Pastor with Dr. Smith. Rev. George B. Patch then carried forward the preparatory work securing an organization as a Church May 9, 1875. The committee constituting this were Dr. J. C. Smith, Dr. J. Chester and Elder D. McFarlan. Mr. Patch was installed November 1, 1875. The number of members was 33. Mr. F. C. Cate and L. Chappel were elected Ruling Elders.

After the resignation in 1881 by Rev. Mr. Patch to enter on his work for the Unity Church, Rev. S. S. Wallen received from the Presbytery of Otsego, New York, was installed April 10 of the year following, and continued with the Church until the autumu of 1883.

The present Pastor, Rev. Eugene Peck, was received from the Presbytery of Otsego, New York, February, 4 1884, and installed over the Church on the 13th of that month. The active membership numbers 80; the Sabbath-School roll shows an average attendance of 350; its teachers and officers number 35, its infant school, under Mrs. S. J. Vaughan, averages 100. Three missionary societies are in progress: two under the ladies, and one sustained by the Sabbath-School scholars. A society among the young people holds weekly meetings for worship and for the study of the Scriptures.

With these activities in Church work and an increased attendance in a still rapidly growing section of the city, the congregation are looking forward in the hopes of a successful effort to erect a house of worship sufficient to accommodate a needy population. Their present building is not only too straitened but frail and uncomfortable; their lots are ample and eligibly located.

OFFICERS.—*Pastor*, Rev. Eugene Peck. *Elder*, F. C. Cate.

Unity Church, 1884.

In September, 1881, meetings for divine service were held in Clabaugh Hall, 14th Street, between Corcoran and R Streets. These grew out of the need of a Presbyterian Church in this rapidly growing section of the city ; some of the Christian brethren appreciating this being Dr. W. H. H. Warman, Major J. T. Power, J. H. Thompson, Emerson Hodges, J. P. Tustin, J. McLeod and B. F. Brochett, who, with their families, sustained the meetings unanimously, inviting Rev. G. B. Patch to take up the new enterprise March 15, 1882 ; a church of 50 members was organized. It asked no aid from the Board of Church Erection.

The present edifice, a Chapel 60 x 43 feet, seating 350, and costing with furnishing about $8,000, was erected in 1884, and dedicated November 15 of that year. The size of entire lot is 103 feet by 60. The estimated value of the properties of the Church is $25,000.

The roll of communicants numbers 200 ; of the Sabbath School 350. A full congregation occupies the sitting capacity of the Church. From the beginning of the work here a blessing has evidently rested on the labors of those who have had its interests on their hearts.

The Pastor, until recently, gave his ministry to it while ocenpying a desk in theGovernment service ; within the current year provision has been made by his people for his support while exclusively devoting himself to the Church. . Providential indications point to the day when a larger Church building may be erected on the commodious adjoining lot.

OFFICERS.—*Pastor*, Rev. George B. Patch, 1323 R. Street, north-west. *Elders*: J. H. Thompson, B. F. Brockett, Emerson Hodges, W. H. H. Warman, Sam'l Snow. *Trustees*: A. G. M. Prevost, A. B. Claxton, G. Pike, W. T. Bailey, F. Guy.

Church of the Covenant, Connecticut Avenue and Eighteenth Street.

Within the five years preceding 1885, the northwestern section of Washington very rapidly advanced in population and in the number and character of the new buildings erected, a majority of its residents being of the wealthier class, and among these some of our best Presbyterian people. A Church of our faith and polity was demanded some years indeed before successful movements could be perfected for its erection. In the year just named, prominent members of the New York Avenue Church, among them several Elders, impressed with the ability of that Church to maintain its full success while it should encourage the new enterprise, held with others a conference, believing that if an eligible site should be secured and a Chapel built here, a good and permanent work would be accomplished.

Before seeking an organization, therefore, in the confidence which faith inspires, they erected a Chapel on N Street, on the east side of the edifice of the Church now being built, which first step cost them the sum of $55,000.

Subscriptions were then opened for the Church, and an organization effected under the Presbytery, October 13, 1885.

March 3d, of the year following, a unanimous call was tendered to Rev. Dr. Tennis S. Hamlin, then Pastor of the Mount Auburn Church, Cincinnati, who accepted it, entering on his duties in May and being installed November 9th. From the commencement of Dr. Hamlin's ministry the presence of the Master has been vouchsafed to His work in answer to the consecrated labors and faith of the membership. This increased during the year from 53 to 154, as reported in March, 1887, to which number 25 have been since then added. The activities of the Church are in grateful exercise; among them the Society of Endeavor which includes the benevolent work of the ladies, the Mission on M and Twenty-eighth Streets. The Society of Endeavor, during its first six months, contributed $1,300 to the cause of Missions; the Mission on Twenty-eighth Street, begun under the care of members of the West Street Church, was adopted by the Church in December, 1886 ; an Industrial School is attached to it.

During the Church year, ending March, 1887, the contributions of the Church to the cause of Missions had reached the sum of $2,686, and the total reported under the head of "Congregational " that of $10,462. Among the latest liberal collections, is the sum of $1,350 for Ministerial Relief.

The main edifice, now approaching completion, will have a seating capacity exceeding 1,000 ; it will be ready for occupancy in the autumn of the present year. The building is of Barber stone, a beautiful light-colored material, quarried a few miles above the City, on the Potomac; the trimmings are of Ohio stone, with much carved work. The tower is monumental and will rise 155 feet ; the lantern, with its corridors on the north and south, is covered with dark-colored tiles. The Church interior is of Oak, and is an elaborate system of arches. The size of the whole lot, on which the property is situated, is 155 feet by 80 ; total cost of main building will be about $125,000 ; Church, Chapel and Pastor's Study cover the whole lot.

OFFICERS. *Pastor*, Rev. Tennis S. Hamlin, D. D. *Elders*, William Ballantyne, C. B. Jewell, Admiral E. R. Calhoun, A. R. Quaiffe, Mr. Justice William Strong, Admiral S. P. Carter. *Deacons*, C. W. Bushnell, H. B. McFarland, M. Brodhead, C. B. Shafer. *Trustees*, Mr. Justice William Strong, Mr. Justice S. Matthews, J. E. Fitch, R. Fendall, W. Ballantyne, Admiral S. P. Carter, M. W. Galt, J. G. Hubbard, C. B. Jewell.

Lewinsville Church, Virginia, 1846.

In 1845, a number of families, emigrating from the Northern and Middle States to the county of Fairfax, Virginia, were temporarily supplied with Presbyterian services by Rev. William Maffit, of the Baltimore Presbytery, then conducting a school near Langley. The year following, Commodore Thos. Ap C. Jones, U. S. N., who, with his family and friends had long desired the gathering of a Presbyterian Congregation at Lewinsville, secured the employment of Rev. L. H. Christian, who successfully carried forward Mr. Maffit's work and that of the occasioual preaching by Rev. Drs. Harrison and Tustin. Mr. Christian also collected funds for the erection of a house of worship from friends in the neighboring counties and in the District of Columbia. A Church organization was effected October 17, 1846, and a house of worship dedicated January 3, 1847; its lot being the gift of Mrs. C. M. Ball. Mr. Amzi Coe and Mr. B. Gilbert were the first Elders.

Following Mr. Christian, Mr. J. M. Henry's labors were much blessed by a revival strengthening the Church; he was succeeded in 1849 by Rev. B. F. Whaley. In 1854, Rev. B. F. Bittinger was elected Pastor, remaining with the Church from October 27, 1851, to January 15, 1857, during which time a large number of additions were made to the membership, and a neat Manse built on ground donated by Mrs. C. M. and Miss Lucy Ball.

The pastorate of Rev. C. B. Makie followed from 1857 to 1859, and the Church enjoyed further prosperity under that of Rev. E. B. Smith, November 10, 1859, to April 13, 1861, when he was dismissed to the Central Presbytery, Phila. The breaking out of the war arrested all; the building and the Manse were occupied by the Union troops under Gen'l Hancock.

From June, 1866, to 1870, Rev. H. P. Dechert regathered the congregation in connection with like services at Falls Church. In 1871, Rev. D. H. Riddle further restored the Church, which, however, was again weakened by the withdrawal, in 1873, of those who were organized into the new Church at "Falls Church" village. On the withdrawal of Mr. Riddle to this last-named organization in 1873, Rev. John Brown was elected Pastor of the Lewinsville and Vienna Churches, the last named being then organized. Mr. Brown was followed in 1875 by Rev. J. Odell, and he, in 1876, by Revs. E. H. Cumpston and S. Murdock as Stated Supplies. In 1882, Rev. H. Clark was installed Pastor. The Church becoming again vacant in 1848 was supplied till August 29, 1886, by Rev. J. E. Nourse, when the present Pastor, Rev. W. H. Edwards, entered on his duties, and was installed October 12 of that year.

The earnest efforts of the congregation and its friends during the last three years have succeeded in restoring the Church buildings, the Manse, and the grounds of the cemetery; and at present the spiritual state of the congregation is one of much promise, the membership having recently more than doubled.

OFFICERS: *Pastor*, Rev. W. H. Edwards; *Elders*, A. J. Head A. Mankin, R. S. Bonham.

Falls Church, February, 1873.

As early as 1812 a committee of the Baltimore Presbytery reported to that body that " three places southwest of the Potomac invited attention," and Professor Maffit, then a member of the Presbytery, was directed to devote as much of his time as possible to these: they were Falls Church, Centre (Centreville), and Difficult. Mr. Maffit had previously supplied the Bladensburg Church, and was afterwards, for some years, engaged in teaching in Fairfax county, Virginia. He died in 1828.

No other work appears, however, to have been done for these places except the holding of the occasional services by Mr. Maffit, until after the lapse of more than twenty years an emigration from the Northern States made it possible to renew preaching services with the hope of establishing permanent good. In 1843, such an emigration took place. It came from the States of Connecticut, New York and Pennsylvania, and was made up of sturdy and industrious families of Presbyterian and Congregational ideas, bringing always, as Bancroft affirms, with them a vigorous element of success. Their first efforts were (as has already been shown) for the vicinity of Lewinsville. Two years later than the establishing of the Lewinsville Church, 1846, a congregation was gathered in the house of the late Mr. Amzi Coe, near the village of Falls Church—a name given to the settlement from its vicinity to the Great Falls of the Potomac. Occasional services were held in this residence and in others near by, which took soon the form of regular Sabbath worship twice a month in Mr. Coe's, until the building of a school house in the village, when under the Pastor of Lewinsville Church, Dr. B. F. Bittinger, for three years, until 1861, these were increased to regular Sabbath-day worship, and under him who then resided there, were attended by the ingathering of a number of members for the Lewinsville Church. In 1861 the war suspended all. Some of the original families, among them those of Mr. Bittinger, Messrs. Coe, Lounsbury, Osborn and Munson had remained in the county. By their efforts Groot Hall, which had been previously occupied for divine service, was soon purchased and fitted up for more permanent use as a church, the securing of which was effected by the vigorous efforts chiefly of the ladies of the congregation, among whom should be named with others, Mrs. R. Bittinger and Miss Lucy Munson (now Mrs. Dr. Taylor, of Wooster, Ohio), who obtained sufficient aid from friends in the Washington churches and in the North to free this hall from debt. It was dedicated November 30, 1866, Rev. Dr. J. Chester preaching the dedication sermon.

Rev. H. P. Dechert, a licentiate of New York Presbytery, had regathered a congregation and ministered to it in connection with his services to the Lewisville Church.

In 1870, Mr. Dechert was succeeded by Rev. David Riddle, who was installed as Pastor of Lewinsville, April 25, 1871. In February, 1873, the members of that church who resided in and near Falls Church were organized in a church of that name, when Mr. Riddle withdrew from Lewinsville, devoting his time to the new organization, and soon after to preaching also at Ballston, where a branch of the Falls Church was formed, and a house of worship erected. It was dedicated October 22d, 1876.

The first Elders elected for Falls Church were Messrs. A. E. Lounsbury, S. A. Coe, M. C. Munson and A. P. Douglas, who continue to serve as such with Mr. W. J. Allen; Messrs. Munson and Douglas at the Ballston Church. In the year 1865, a handsome gothic stone edifice, 52 feet by 32, with a tower, was completed at Falls Church.

The dedicatory services were conducted October 30th by Rev.

Drs. Bartlett and Bittinger, the historical memorial being by the Pastor. The value of this property, of the building first ocenpied and of the Ballston Church, is estimated at $16,000.

The roll of members reported to the Assembly of 1887 numbers 110; of Sabbath-School scholars, 144. The columns of contributions to the Boards of the Church, are well filled and the activities of the members are largely enlisted in the various objects of church work.

OFFICERS.—*Pastor*, Rev. D. H. Riddle. *Elders:* M. C. Munson, A. E. Lounsbury, S. A. Coe, A. P. Douglas, W. J. Allen. *Trustees:* For Falls Church—D. O. Munson, G. B. Ives, Seth Osborne, G. O. Mankin; For Ballston—H. O. Whallon, —— Clemens, A. G. Hays.

Vienna Presbyterian Church, 1873,

was organized November 16, 1873, by Rev. J. G. Hamner, Synodical Missionary, by authority of the Presbytery of Washington city. Its nine first members were those whose names had been first enrolled on the session book of the Lewinsville Church, but who now desired to revive the state of religion in their immediate neighborhood, there being no house of worship for the county on a line between Lewinsville and Fairfax Court-House. The war had suspended the occasional services which had been held by the Presbyterian Ministers at this village. Through the efforts of Rev. John Brown, then Pastor of the Church at Lewinsville, supported by the liberal contributions of Messrs. Kenyon, Van Orden, Head, and others in the vicinity, and with aid from the Board of Church Erection, and of friends in Washington, a neat Church edifice was erected in 1873, and Mr. Brown was installed Pastor, remaining with the Church until 1875. He was succeeded by Rev. J. Odell, as stated supply for one year, following whom were Revs. S. Murdock and E. H. Cumpston. In 1882 Rev. H. Clark was installed, and continued until August, 1884, when the Church, becoming again vacant, was supplied until August, 1886, by Rev. J. E. Nourse. The present Pastor, Rev. W. H. Edwards, was installed October 29, 1886.

The Church is young in years, and consists of those who are in but moderate circumstances, but whose desires are toward the upbuilding of the Kingdom. It is under careful oversight, and promises permanent good to the homes of its people, and a decided influence on the community. During the past three years ground has been purchased for a Manse, and other improvements added.

OFFICERS.—*Pastor*, Rev. William H. Edwards; *Elders*, B. W. Head, J. R. Blake, H. C. Powell, A. B. Shaw.

First Prince William Church, Virginia, 1850, Manassas Church, Clifton Church.

The accounts of these Churches, originally in the same missionary field, are taken chiefly from the journal of Dr. B. F. Bittinger. The field in which they were organized—the two first in Prince William county, and the last in Fairfax county—has been for the most part served as one.

First Prince William Church.

Before the year 1848 occasional services had been held in private houses in the vicinity of the present settlement of Nokesville by Rev. Dr. Harrison, of the Alexandria Church, and Rev. Mr. Stoddert, of the Winchester Presbytery. In 1848 the families of Messrs. Hornbaker and Rube, and other Presbyterians, having removed there from New Jersey and Pennsylvania, the Presbytery of Winchester at their request appointed Rev. J. M. Henry to organize a Church, which was effected July 20, 1850.

Following Mr. Henry the services were further well sustained, chiefly by Rev. Thomas Balch, until the outbreak of the war, which scattered the Northern people and closed the Church. The building was saved from the flames of war by the intercession of Mrs. Mary Kline, one of its members.

In the fall of 1866, at the request of the people to have the services renewed by the Presbytery of Potomac, Rev. J. E. Nourse resumed preaching in the dwelling of Mrs. Rube, and in the spring which followed the building was repaired. Its grounds and the cemetery lot were the donation of Mr. Thatcher, of New Jersey. In 1875 Rev. Mr. Carmichael became the Stated Supply, and was succeeded in 1878 by Rev. Mr. F. M. Todd, the present pastor of the Manassas Church. No pastorate has existed. The population of the neighborhood has rather declined than increased, and there is apparently little, if any, of a new element to maintain Presbyterian services. Membership, 16.

Elders.—John Slaught, W. S. Swayzee, J. G. Reading.

Manassas Church

was organized soon after the close of the war, from the sufferings of which it was reviving. It had destroyed nearly every dwelling in the town. Members of the First Prince William Church residing near the old town, and having had their own house of worship near there destroyed by the war, petitioned the Potomac Presbytery for a new organization, and this was effected by a committee consisting of Revs. John Chester and J. E. Nourse, July 6, 1867. The first Elders were Messrs. G. W. Mitchell and Levi H. Newman. An advantageous lot having been purchased in the centre of the town, by the self-denial and assistance of a few members, and by help from friends abroad, a brown freestone house of worship was erected after services in a small frame building for several years. From 1867 Rev. J. E. Nourse was the Stated Supply until 1875, when Mr. Carmichael took charge of this and the Prince William congregation. In 1878, Rev. Mr. Todd was installed Pastor.

The roll of church members numbers 61; Sabbath-school roll, 57. The contributions to the Boards are well maintained.

OFFICERS:—*Pastor*, Rev. F. M. Todd; *Elders*, C. A. Snowball, C. H. Worthington, G. Trimmer, E. Goode, O. Chamberlain.

Clifton Church, Fairfax County, Virginia.

In 1868, Mr. Harrison G. Otis, of Geneva, N. Y., and not long afterwards Messrs. J. Sanford Otis and H. C. Newman, of Orange, and T. B. Graham, of Montclair, N. J., having removed to this section, began some stated Sabbath services for the people of the neighborhood, and looked for the establishment of a Presbyterian Church.

Rev. J. E. Nourse, then supplying the First Prince William and Manassas field, held for them the first regular services in the basement of a then unfinished building owned by Mr. H. G. Otis.

The ground for a church, with an additional liberal contribution, having been given by Mr. H. G. and Mrs. Mary Otis, and help being secured from the Board of Church Erection and from friends, by Mr. Newman and J. S. Otis, chiefly in Brooklyn, the corner-stone was laid December 31, 1871; an organization having been effected in May previous. Rev. William Bradley, removing to this place from New York, became the Stated Supply until 1877, when Rev. Mr. Todd, of Manassas, succeeded in con nection with the Manassas Church.

Since 1881 the pulpit has been supplied by appointments under Presbytery, chiefly by Rev. Dr. Dudley and the late Charles H. Raymond. The Church edifice has been recently fully repaired by the liberal efforts of a small congregation, aided by friends in Maryland. The enterprise properly belongs to the same field with the Manassas and First Prince William Churches, with which it may become self-sustaining. Attendance on the stated services is good and the Sabbath-School work is encouraging for the Church and for the village. Its roll numbers 61.

OFFICERS:—*Elders*, H. C. Newman, T. B. Graham, W. E. Ford·

Darnestown Church, Montgomery County, Md.

Previous to 1850, for several years, Rev. Charles H. Nourse gave much ministerial labor to this region, preaching at Middlebrook, Darnestown, and Poolesville, at which last-named place he gathered a congregation and secured the erection of the present church building.

The Darnestown Church grew out of the labors of Rev. Daniel Motzer while laboring as a domestic missionary in Montgomery county under the direction of the Presbytery of Baltimore and supported by the Churches—Bridge street, Georgetown, and F street, Washington city—and by Mrs. Fitzgerald, of Virginia. Mr. Motzer commenced his labors in Neelsville Sept. 1, 1854, devoting a part of his time to the vicinity of Darnestown. At first he held worship in an old log building at Pleasant Hill, known as the "Union Church." This was in May, 1855. His labors were greatly blessed, and it was not long before the way was opened for the erection of a Presbyterian Church near the village of Darnestown. Mrs. John F. Du Fief generously donated three acres of ground for the purpose, and on the 14th of September, 1855, the corner-stone of the present building was laid with appropriate religious services by Rev. Mr. Motzer, aided by Rev. Dr. Gurley, of Washington city. April, 1857, Messrs. J. Darby and J. C. Dellet were elected Ruling Elders. At the close of the first year the number of communicants had increased to forty-five, the larger number on profession, and Mr. Motzer's labors continued to receive the Divine blessing till his death,

March 1, 1864. He was succeeded by Rev. J. S. H. Henderson as Stated Supply, 1864–1870. Rev. Chas. Beach serving the Church from Dec. 10, 1870, was installed Oct. 30, 1871, and continned till Sept. 17, 1877. and was succeeded by Rev. H. C. Brown as Stated Supply March 3, 1878. In 1883 Rev. James M. Nourse was elected Pastor and installed Nov. 14, remaining with the people until April 27, 1885. He was succeeded by Rev. Davis . L. Rathbun, of the Baltimore Presbytery; installed October 28, 1885. The roll of members reported to the Assembly numbers eighty. Columns for contributions to the Boards of the Church, all filled.

OFFICERS.—Rev. D. L. Rathbun; *Elders*, F. A. Tschiffely, M. B. Montgomery, J. S. Winder, Thomas Kelly, and Geo. R. Rice.

Neelsville Church, Montgomery County, Maryland.

This organization was made December 6, 1845, by the Rev. Elias Harrison, D. D., and Rev. John Miller, a committee of the Presbytery of Baltimore. Its members were formerly connected with the church at Rockville. Mr. Wm. Musser was their first Ruling Elder. For two years the Church was supplied by the Rev. Samuel J. Baird, who was succeeded by Rev. A. M. Hershey.

September 1, 1854, Rev. Daniel Motzer connected his charge of the Darnestown Church with his ministerial labors here, and remained with the people till his death, March 1, 1864.

Rev. James S. H. Henderson supplied the pulpit from 1864 to 1870 in connection with the supply of the Darnestown Church; from May, 1870, until his death he preached at Neelsville only. From the time of his death the pulpit has been supplied by members of the Washington City Presbytery; for three years by Rev. J. L. French. The Church has never had a pastorate.

The Moderator of the Session is Rev. T. S. Childs, D. D. The first house of worship, built in 1842, was replaced by a more commodious one in June, 1878.

Elders, 1887.—J. T. Warfield, J. E. Deets, W. Musser, W. T. Lewis.

Boyd's Station.

The Church here was the result of the labors of Rev. J. S. H. Henderson, while laboring also at Neelsville. Its house of worship was dedicated in June, 1876. No pastorate has been formed. The Moderator of the Session, since the date of supply by Rev· J. L. French, is Dr. T. S. Childs.

Elders, 1887.—J. A. Boyd, M. T. Lewis.

Hermon Church, 1874.

This Church, nine miles distant from Georgetown, is the inheritor of one of the very earliest of Presbyterian organization in this region, the Cabin John Church, founded by Rev. Hugh Conn, already named as having founded the Old Bladensburg organization of 1718. Cabin John was organized in 1752, the last year of Mr. Conn's Ministry. At the first meeting of Baltimore Presbytery, 1786, Rev. James Hunt represented the Church, and in 1809, Rev. John Breckenridge supplied the pulpit in connection with his ministry to the first Presbyterian Church of Washington. The remains of Rev. Mr. Hunt were interred near the church building, some of the timbers of which may still be seen. In 1823, Rev. John Mines supplied the Church in connection with his charge of Rockville, and at times Bethesda. This organization, however, became extinct, the property being also lost by its transfer to another people.

Through the efforts of Mr. J. W. D. Moore, formerly a member of the West Street Church, Georgetown, a new organization was effected January 5, 1874, under Rev. Dr. S. H. Howe and Rev. J. G. Hamner, Jr. Mr. Hamner had been for some months, holding services in an adjacent school house. In November of the same year, a neat frame building, erected by the residents of the neighborhood, with, aid also from our Board of Church Erection, and firm friends in West Street Church, was dedicated. Since that date, with the exception of the two years' supply of the pulpit, by Rev. John A. Carmichael, in connection with his services also at Manassas, Virginia, the Church has been almost continuously cared for by Rev. Dr. T. W. Simpson. It is in an isolated location, making it difficult for a small congregation to maintain its services. The report to the Assembly of 1887, was that of 29 members, and 30 Sabbath-School Scholars. Elders J. D. W. Moore and R. G. Davidson.

For aid in carrying forward the typographical execution of this volume, I am indebted to my young friend Mr. C. T. Bell, printer, 1530 29th street N W.